# F☆U☆B☆A☆R

SAM SEDER & STEPHEN SHERRILL

# F★U★B★A★R

## AMERICA'S RIGHT-WING
## NIGHTMARE

HarperCollins*Publishers*

HarperCollins books may be purchased for educational, business, or sales promotional use. For information, please write: Special Markets Department, HarperCollins Publishers, 10 East 53rd Street, New York, NY 10022.

FIRST EDITION

*Designed by Laura Lindgren*

Printed on acid-free paper

Library of Congress Cataloging-in-Publication Data is available upon request.

ISBN-10: 0-06-084671-2
ISBN-13: 978-0-06-084671-8

06   07   08   09   10    LLD/RRD   10   9   8   7   6   5   4   3   2   1

Sam:
*To Nikki and Myla*

Stephen:
*To Cate*

# CONTENTS

# INTRODUCTION

"F.U.B.A.R." is a military acronym that means **FUCKED UP BEYOND ALL RECOGNITION**. It is the authors' contention that the country has been fucked up. But more than just the general "boy, things are really fucked up" feeling that most Americans have when watching the news or rolling their eyes at the "more-'partisan-bickering'-by-those-Washington-politicians" tone the media takes with any story about politics.

This is a different kind of fucked up—one that's making America unrecognizable as the America most Americans feel they know. You may think the political and social situation in this country is bad. But it's worse. It's the Rapture Right Paradox: to whatever extent you realize Bush and the Rapture Right have fucked America up, it's *always* worse. However worse you think it is, it's worser. So far, scientists have been unable to come up with a successful mathematical proof of the Rapture Right Paradox, but then the Rapture Right isn't so big on science.

How have they been able to fuck things up so badly? It's sort of like those parasites who eat their host from the inside without the host even knowing—keeping them alive for as long as possible. Everything looks normal until the host is no longer needed, and then, poof—it all crumbles. They depend on you being, essentially, asleep and unaware of what's going on.

Sure, you've been up, walking around, spending money, eating stuff, signing for packages, lifting babies, handling glass things, grilling meats; but you've been asleep.

Maybe it was Bill Clinton who put you to sleep. Maybe it was a good run of a tech stock. Maybe it was the media's obsession with missing white women. Maybe it was the job, the kids, Ben and Jen or Jen and Brad. Maybe it was the *arrivé* of the Beaujolais nouveau. Maybe you follow politics, maybe you're liberal or independent or Democrat or fiscally responsible or progressive or intelligent—probably most of these things. But you've been asleep.

Nothing to be ashamed of. We realize people have lives to lead, families to take care of. And sometimes it's easier to just go along, and not want to know too much about what's going on. We have these tendencies, too—we're both meat-eaters, for example, though suspect we wouldn't be if we delved too deeply into how that hamburger wound up on our plate at the Corner Bistro.

But, you say, I know the country is having a tough time, I know the Bush administration is corrupt, I know about Tom DeLay and Jack Abramoff, I know about the lies before the war started and the lies after the war started, I know about the trillion-dollar Iraq War bill my grandkids will have to pay, I know about the huge deficits, the wage stagnation, the hackery and incompetence exposed by Katrina, the secret NSA domestic spying with no court order.

But that's not all the right wing is doing. They're not just trying to reshape the political landscape of the country; they're trying to redefine things like reality and truth. They'll take the former where they can get it (and they've gotten a lot of it during the last five years), but it's the latter where the chance for big, wholesale change is.

That's why, as you'll notice, we use the terms "Bush," "Republicans," and "Rapture Right" interchangeably. What was once the fringe—the embarrassing cousin they saw only when they had to (special occasions, especially the ones held every four years in November)—has now become the heart of the Republican Party. They've finally got the real power, and, like Bush with the phantom "political capital" he claimed to have earned after the 2004 election, they intend to use it.

So, while Bush chips away at the outside, the Rapture Right chips away at the foundation. A little bit of doubt about the truth of evolution here, a little bit of social security lies there, a little bit of fear about homosexuals everywhere, and pretty soon the country's all fucked up.

Among other things,* *F.U.B.A.R.* serves as an attempt to show you how they're doing this, wake you up to the nightmare that is Rapture Right America, and give you a few pointers about how to live more comfortably in the New America.

To those out there who may feel they're not ready to experience the full awakening, we've thought of you, too. For you we've included a lot of fun puzzles and games that you can skip to if you'd rather not see what's going on. They can be found at the end of the book—so if you choose to avail yourself of this option, you, too, can feel like you've "finished" the book.

But we hope the rest of you will press on. If you don't, then the Rapture Right has won. We're fighting them here so you don't have to fight them . . . oh well . . .

---

* Like, say, a paperweight, a "re-gift," a historical document that will help future generations understand what led to the "riots of 2009," a carefully hidden coded Scientology recruitment message, et cetera.

# F☆U☆B☆A☆R

# 1 · TALIBAN DREAMIN'

## THE BAD NEWS IS THERE'S NO GOOD NEWS

You may have noticed that under the Bush regime the line between church and state has gotten a bit blurry. Maybe you've heard about a Ten Commandment controversy here or an attorney general anointing himself with cooking oil there.* Perhaps you know that over the past five years your government has given more than a billion dollars of your tax money to tax-exempt churches for "faith-based initiatives" ( aka "pay-Yah-weh-ola"). Perhaps you've been following the brouhaha over trying to change the Constitution so that gay people can't get married. But hey, no biggie, they're doing their thing, I'm doing mine.

The problem is that your thing *is* their thing. The Republican Party isn't the charming, noblesse-oblige, country-club avuncular-drunk Grand Old Party of yesteryear. There's a new sheriff in GOP town. One who believes we're living in end times. This one is lighter on the charm and

---

* It was Crisco. We'll explain later.

heavier on the apocalypse. He's a Rapture Republican, a Big Government Theocrat, a Radical Cleric—an American Taliban.

If you're reading this book, chances are you're a thoughtful, curious person. In our new future under Rapture Republican rule, you may want to think about dialing that kind of thing down a bit. When in public, stick to simple declarative sentences, like, "Hey, that's tall!" or *"According to Jim* was awesome last night!" If the world looks flat from where you are, it's flat.

As far as reading in particular, scale back quickly (after, of course, you finish reading this book). If you feel like you absolutely must continue reading, pick up a *People* or *Us Weekly* (*Time* and *Newsweek* work just as well). Nothing will make you more docile than having your head filled with the details of Nick and Jessica's divorce or whether it's Hilary or Lindsay who's being the jerk about the whole thing.*

☆ ☆ ☆

## RETURN TO THE WORLD THAT NEVER WAS

Sure the Rapture Right has always been around, but the new reality is that Washington—and statehouses and school boards and newsrooms around the country—are flooded with them. What was once funny† is no longer so funny. Ever wonder why you don't hear much about the Christian Coalition or the Moral Majority anymore? Well, they've changed their names—now they're just called Republicans. Here's Hanna Rosin writing in the *Washington Post* in March 2005:

> This year evangelicals in public office have finally become so numer-
> ous that they've blended in to the permanent Washington backdrop, a
> new establishment that has absorbed the local habits and mores . . .

---

* It's so Lindsay.

† E.g., Tammy Faye Bakker, with all that crazy makeup!

And a lot of them have already absorbed the local habits and mores of Capitol Hill:

> . . . Nearly every third congressional office stocks an ambitious Christian leader who calls himself "evangelical," according to Jim Guth, a political science professor at Furman University.*

Coral Ridge Ministries boasts a weekly television show and a daily radio show broadcast to millions. The following was written by its former executive director George Grant.† It's basically the mission statement of the Rapture Right:

> Christians have an obligation, a mandate, a commission, a holy responsibility to reclaim the land for Jesus Christ—to have dominion in the civil structures, just as in every other aspect of life and godliness. But it is dominion that we are after. Not just a voice. It is dominion we are after. Not just influence. It is dominion we are after. Not just equal time. It is dominion we are after.
>
> World conquest. That's what Christ has commissioned us to accomplish. We must win the world with the power of the Gospel. And we must never settle for anything less. If Jesus Christ is indeed Lord, as the Bible says, and if our commission is to bring the land into subjection to His Lordship, as the Bible says, then all our activities, all our witnessing, all our preaching, all our craftsmanship, all our stewardship, and all our political action will aim at nothing short of that sacred purpose. Thus, Christian politics has as its primary intent the conquest of the land—of men, families, institutions, bureaucracies, courts, and governments for the Kingdom of Christ. It is to reinstitute the

---

* "Right with God: Evangelical Conservatives Find a Spiritual Home on the Hill," Hanna Rosin, *Washington Post,* March 6, 2005, page D01.

† From his book *The Changing of the Guard: Biblical Principles for Political Action* (Fort Worth, Texas: Dominion Press, 1987).

authority of God's Word as supreme over all judgments, over all legislation, over all declarations, constitutions, and confederations.*

Why should they have dominion over all the creatures of the Earth? Because that's what it says in the Bible: "And God said, Let us make man in our image, after our likeness: and let them have dominion over the fish of the sea, and over the fowl of the air, and over the cattle, and over all the earth, and over every creeping thing that creepeth upon the earth" (Genesis 1:26). There thou hath it: if thou creepeth, lo, do they hath dominion over thee!

They want it all. And it's not just geographic dominion. While the press has reasonably been distracted with the right's attempt at dominion over the Middle East, they've set about locking up dominion over the homefront—over sex, religion, your finances (which is to say, your future), and over science. Those are what we're going to focus on, and not just because we don't want to go to Iraq.†

It's the last of those—science—that we'll start with. Because it's really a battle over truth itself, and they realize that if they can win that, then their "domino theory" may work after all.

---

*  Ibid.

†  We would, but we're pretty sure they wouldn't let us in the Green Zone.

# 2 · OPEN YOUR MIND

"In a child's ability to master the multiplication table, there is more holiness than all your shouted hosannas and holy holies. An idea is more important than a monument, and the advancement of Man's knowledge more miraculous than all the sticks turned to snakes and the parting of the waters."—*Inherit the Wind*

Turns out, an idea is not just more important than a monument, it's more important than a fact.

Intelligent design is the new smart bomb of the religious right. It may not be science, but it's still brilliant. For a long time, religion and science coexisted pretty well. There was that dustup with Galileo, and the Scopes glitch, but, for the most part, science was science, religion was religion.

The genius of the intelligent-design concept, though, is how it uses the principles of enlightenment and progressivism to destroy . . . enlightenment and progressivism.

And that's because with the new version, Intelligent Design 2.0, all its proponents are asking for is "open-mindedness," to "have a debate," to "consider all sides." Science is hard stuff—that's why you usually need a Ph.D. to be a scientist. But the intelligent-design crowd has been able to turn that into a plus, by conflating complexity with "contradiction." And all they're asking is for schools to "present both sides."

As Senator Rick Santorum told the *Washington Post* on March 14,

2005, "My reading of the science is there's a legitimate debate. My feeling is let the debate be had."

One might argue that we had that debate. Most notably, in the seventeenth century. And later there was even a whole play about it. Or you may have thought the new debate over the "debate" was settled in November 2005, when members of a local school board in Dover, Pennsylvania, were voted out over their requirement that intelligent design be taught in the classroom, and the subsequent decision by a federal judge that ruled the requirement unconstitutional. Just a small bump in the road for intelligent design. They've been waiting a few hundred years for this, and a few liberal jerk-offs in Dover, Pennsylvania, won't stop them.

In fact, in March 2005, a statewide law was proposed in Pennsylvania:

House Bill 1007:

Section 1516.2. Teaching Theories on the Origin of Man and Earth.—(a) In any public school instruction concerning the theories of the origin of man and the earth which includes the theory commonly known as evolution, a board of school directors may include, as a portion of such instruction, the theory of intelligent design. Upon approval of the board of school directors, any teacher may use supporting evidence deemed necessary for instruction on the theory of intelligent design.

And various intelligent-design "alternatives" are currently being considered in thirty states.*

As Eugenie C. Scott of the National Center for Science Education told the *Washington Post*, "The energy level is new. The religious right had an effect nationally [in the election]. Now, by golly, they want to call in the chits."

And they are, pushed by groups like the Discovery Institute, which bills itself as "a nonpartisan public policy think tank conducting research

---

* "Academics Consider 'Intelligent Design' Museum Talk," Christopher Michaud, Reuters News Service, December 5, 2005.

on technology, science and culture, economics and foreign affairs," but which spends more than $1 million a year promoting intelligent design.*

In the summer of 2005, President Bush himself said: "Both sides ought to be properly taught . . . so people can understand what the debate is about."

Some thought the debate was at least settled within the Catholic Church, which had seemed to make its peace with Darwin. Pope John Paul II had declared in 1992 that the whole Galileo thing was a "tragic mutual incomprehension," and in 1996 said that evolution was "more than just a hypothesis."

Not so fast. In a July 2005 *New York Times* op-ed piece, the influential Austrian cardinal Christoph Schoenhorn dismissed John Paul's statement as "rather vague and unimportant," and said that "evolution in the neo-Darwinian sense" (whatever that "neo" means) is "not true."

Then, in November, Pope Benedict XVI, expressing solidarity with his American counterpart in the White House, quoted Saint Basil the Great, a fourth-century saint who warned about those "fooled by the atheism that they carry inside of them, imagine a universe free of direction and order, as if at the mercy of chance."

And if that's not clear enough, Benedict clarified:

How many of these people are there today? These people, "fooled by atheism," believe and try to demonstrate that it's scientific to think that everything is free of direction and order . . .

With the sacred Scripture, the Lord awakens the reason that sleeps and tells us: In the beginning, there was the creative word. In the beginning, the creative word—this word that created everything and created this intelligent project that is the cosmos—is also love.

"Intelligent project"? Hmmm. That sounds familiar.

And, of course, there's Kansas. Always Kansas. On the same day as the vote in Dover took place, the statewide Kansas Board of Education voted six to four to include challenges to Darwin in school curricula.

---

* "Battle on Teaching Evolution Sharpens," Peter Slevin, *Washington Post*, March 14, 2005, page A01.

But again, it was just because they agreed with the liberal principles of open-mindedness. Kenneth Willard, a board member who supported the changes, accused the scientific establishment of having a "blind faith in evolution" and a "high degree of fear of change." Steve Abrams, the board chairman, said the changes simply meant "more science" would be taught.

They know the history of Kansas and evolution, and they know the changes were late-night-monologue-joke magnets. But look how carefully the changes are worded. It's all about the "full range" of views:

> Regarding the scientific theory of biological evolution, the curriculum standards call for students to learn about the best evidence for modern evolutionary theory, but also to learn about areas where scientists are raising scientific criticisms of the theory.
>
> These curriculum standards reflect the Board's objective of:
> 1) to help students understand the full range of scientific views that exist on this topic.
> 2) to enhance critical thinking and the understanding of the scientific method by encouraging students to study different and opposing scientific evidence.
> 3) to ensure that science education in our state is "secular, neutral, and non-ideological."*

Notice that last bit. See? This is secular. It's not about God . . . per se, just *something*, wink wink—who put it all together. Don't be so uptight. Have an "open mind":

> The Board has heard credible scientific testimony that indeed there are significant debates about the evidence for key aspects of chemical and biological evolutionary theory.
>
> All scientific theories should be approached with an open mind, studied carefully, and critically considered. We therefore think it is

---

* Kansas State Board of Education, November 8, 2005.

important and appropriate for students to know about these scientific debates and for the Science Curriculum Standards to include information about them.*

In fact, they're not even mandating intelligent design at all:

> We also emphasize that the Science Curriculum Standards do not include Intelligent Design, the scientific disagreement with the claim of many evolutionary biologists that the apparent design of living systems is an illusion.

Notice the word "apparent." Apparently, it's settled in Kansas that the "design" of living systems is "apparent." And they're not saying ID must be taught—that would be the old MO. Now they're only asking that alternative views of evolution be taught . . . the only one of which is . . . intelligent design.

All this respect for "open-mindedness" is working. Polls show that the large majority of Americans believe man was created by God alone, and a Gallup poll showed in March 2005 that 38 percent of teens ages thirteen to eighteen believe that "God created human beings pretty much in their present form at one time within the last 10,000 years," while 43 percent believe that "human beings have developed over millions of years from less advanced forms of life, but God guided this process." The number who believe that man developed over millions of years without God's guidance—18 percent.

This is a typical quote. It comes from a twenty-one-year-old named Hannah Maxon—who also happens to be a math and chemistry major at Cornell and the founder of Cornell's Intelligent Design and Evolution Awareness (IDEA) club:

> In my opinion, both intelligent design and Darwinian evolution are science. Both have philosophical implications. Intelligent design implies

---

* Ibid.

the universe is somewhat directed. Darwinian evolution implies a naturalistic worldview.

And, according to the National Science Teachers Association, 31 percent of science teachers "feel pressured to include creationism, intelligent design, or other nonscientific alternatives to evolution in their science classroom."* As Gary Wheeler, executive director of the NSTA, puts it: "A teacher's job is to foster a deep understanding of science in students and help them better understand the natural world around us. But something is not right when science educators feel pressure to teach a variety of religious or non-science viewpoints. It's not fair to our students to give them anything less than good science."

They're not the only ones who are apparently intimidated. On October 6, 2005, the *New York Times* published a piece by Jodi Wilgoren, called "Seeing Creation and Evolution in Grand Canyon." Jodi was also very open-minded—to the point of giving her readers a completely distorted picture of the relative credibility of each side. Here's how she laid it out:

> Geologists date this sandstone to 550 million years ago and explain the folding as a result of pressure from shifting faults underneath. But to Mr. Vail, the folds suggest the Grand Canyon was carved 4,500 years ago by the great global flood described in Genesis as God's punishment for humanity's sin.

And that was pretty much the tone throughout. Present both sides, draw no conclusions. The piece was immediately attacked, most notably by the blog Pharyngula. They e-mailed Jodi, and she e-mailed right back:

> I don't consider myself a creationist. I don't have any interest in sharing my personal views on how the canyon was carved, mostly because I've

---

* "Survey Indicates Science Teachers Feel Pressure to Teach Nonscientific Alternatives to Evolution," Press Release, National Science Teachers Association, March 24, 2005.

spent almost no time pondering my personal views—it takes all my energy as a reporter and writer to understand and explain my subjects' views fairly and thoroughly.

Well, as long as you explain their views thoroughly. Too bad there wasn't just a little bit of energy left over to explain that her "subjects' views" aren't equally credible.

The anti-evolutionists, it turns out, have a lot more energy than Jodi. This summer, owners of several IMAX theaters around the country canceled showings of the movie *Volcanoes*—an IMAX film about, uh, volcanoes—because of objections from the anti-evolution folks—i.e., the "open-minded people who just want to hear all sides."

According to one of those who rejected the movie, Lisa Buzzelli, director of an IMAX theater in Charleston, South Carolina, "We've got to pick a film that's going to sell in our area. If it's not going to sell, we're not going to take it . . . Many people here believe in creationism, not evolution." Of course, most people don't believe in talking fish, but they still showed *Finding Nemo*.

But, hey, at least we've still got PBS, right? They're onto that, too. *Unlocking the Mysteries of Life*, a "documentary" on intelligent design that forcefully rejects Darwinism, has been aired on PBS stations in Washington, Los Angeles, Miami, and New York.* One station in New Mexico that chose not to air the "documentary"—citing PBS producer's guidelines that "a reasonable segment of the public might readily conclude that the program was created solely to promote the interests of the funder"†— was accused of "censoring science."

Supporters of the "documentary" claimed that it was very scientific— and yet an ad for the film in a missionary newspaper referred to it as "the most impressive evangelistic tool ever made. Using the latest computer

---

* "KNME accused of censorship," KOBTV.com, Reed Upton, January 6, 2005.
† "Albuquerque PBS Station Under Fire by Creationists," Dave Thomas, president, New Mexicans for Science and Reason, Pandasthumb.org, January 7, 2005.

graphics it displays the wisdom of God in the creation of the inner workings of the human cell."*

Of course, all this open-mindedness is really just an opening to a much wider agenda. In 1999, the Discovery Institute's Center for the Renewal of Science and Culture produced an internal memorandum called "The Wedge Document," outlining how the struggle against evolution is part of a much larger campaign:

> The social consequences of materialism have been devastating. As symptoms, those consequences are certainly worth treating. However, we are convinced that in order to defeat materialism, we must cut it off at its source. That source is scientific materialism. This is precisely our strategy. If we view the predominant materialistic science as a giant tree, our strategy is intended to function as a "wedge" that, while relatively small, can split the trunk when applied at its weakest points. The very beginning of this strategy, the "thin edge of the wedge," was Phillip Johnson's critique of Darwinism begun in 1991 in *Darwinism on Trial,* and continued in *Reason in the Balance* and *Defeating Darwinism by Opening Minds.* Michael Behe's highly successful *Darwin's Black Box* followed Johnson's work. *We are building on this momentum, broadening the wedge with a positive scientific alternative to materialistic scientific theories, which has come to be called the theory of intelligent design (ID).*[†]

But here's the money shot:

> Design theory promises to reverse the stifling dominance of the materialist worldview, and to replace it with a science consonant with Christian and theistic convictions.[‡]

---

* Ibid.
† http://www.kcfs.org/Fliers_articles/Wedge.html, and many other places on the Web; italics ours.
‡ Ibid.

Or, in the words of Terry Fox, pastor of the largest Baptist church in the Midwest, "If you can cause enough doubt on evolution, liberalism will die."*

But don't think it's just the Rapture Rightists. There are plenty of right-wingers out there who wouldn't be caught dead actually making an intelligent-design argument themselves, but they're happy to send out the Rapturites to use this new weapon of "open-mindedness" to break down the notion of reality. Once that's accomplished, then they can really get to work.

Here's neocon godmother Gertrude Himmelfarb—wife of Irving Kristol and the woman who gave birth to Bill Kristol—quoted in the *New Republic* from December 2005:

> Today we have even more cause to be concerned about the mechanistic and reductionistic interpretation of all human life, including its emotional and intellectual dimensions, in the name of Darwinism. This is more than science. It is scientism—and scientism with a vengeance, for it is not only science that is now presumed to be the only access to comprehensive truth, but also that sub-category of science known as Darwinism.

So now the reality-based world is "scientism." And, it follows, the thing one would logically call people who believe in this dangerous "scientism" is . . . "scientists" . . . i.e., closed-minded people who discriminate against other ways to access "comprehensive truth."

---

* "Battle on Teaching Evolution Sharpens," Peter Slevin, *Washington Post,* March 14, 2005, page A01.

# INTELLIGENT LAWS OF MOTION

In 1687, Sir Isaac Newton published his *Philosophiae Naturalis Principia Mathematica*, which contained his three laws of motion. Not only was Newton writing in a language nobody could understand, he did not yet have the benefit of knowing about the exciting new breakthroughs in intelligent design, which would occur three hundred years after its publication. Since he would probably be embarrassed about his "laws of motion" in light of these new findings, we've taken the liberty of updating them, in accordance with the scientific laws of intelligent design. (ID-related updates are shown in italics.)

I. Newton's Law of Inertia:

Every object in a state of uniform motion tends to remain in that state of motion unless an external force is applied to it *by something, or someone, since only an intelligent agent of some kind (not*

*necessarily God, but not necessarily not God) could recognize that this object was in motion and decide to "apply" an external force.*

II. Newton's Law of Dynamics: f = m*a $%^&* iangbmg*

Which means: the acceleration (a) of an object is directly proportional to the net force (f) exerted and inversely proportional to the object's mass (m) *is derived from () the wishes of the intelligent agent— not God but maybe God (iangbmg).*

III. Newton's Law of Reciprocal Actions:

For every action there is an equal and opposite reaction, *unless an intelligent agent who may or may not answer to the name of "God" wishes it to be only some actions or not quite equal reaction, or, really, anything else, in which case, it is those things, because he's the designer, and if you don't like it, design your own fucking universe.*

# 3 · ASK MR. SCIENCE GUY

A lot of people think science is intimidating. All those numbers and facts and stuff! But it doesn't have to be. The entire universe works according to certain simple principles. Once you understand these rules, the world around you becomes a much more exciting and fascinating place.

Many people also make the mistake of thinking of science as a bunch of unchanging facts, set in stone by some group of stuffy know-it-alls in white lab coats. But science is a dynamic, ever-shifting discipline. In fact, just in the past few years, there have been many breakthroughs. What we think we "know" is always changing.

Mr. Science Guy is here to provide the answers. And even if you believe you're well grounded in science, "Ask Mr. Science Guy" will put you on the right path.

**Q:** *Where do rainbows come from?*—Eric Bailey, McGregor, Texas

**Mr. Science Guy:** Rainbows aren't just beautiful—they're a wonderful illustration of many fascinating scientific principles. Even though light looks white, it's actually made up of several different colors: red, orange, yellow, green, blue, indigo, and violet. Every material has something called a "refractive index." When light enters a prism, the difference in the refractive index of the glass and the air makes the light bend, and this makes the colors separate.

Accordingly, rainbows are caused because of man's wickedness. You see, Eric, when the earth was created, it was without form, and void; and darkness *was* on the face of the deep. And the spirit of God was hovering over the face of the waters. Then God said, "Let there be light"; and there was light. And God saw the light, that it was good; and God divided the light from the darkness.

But then the Lord saw that the wickedness of man was great in the earth, and that every intent of the thoughts of his heart was only evil continually. And the Lord was sorry that He had made man on the earth, and He was grieved in His heart. So the Lord said, "I will destroy man whom I have created from the face of the earth, both man and beast, creeping thing and birds of the air, for I am sorry that I have made them."

So he did destroy the earth, Eric. He destroyed every living thing with a flood, except for Noah and his family, and the animals that Noah collected on the Ark.

After the water went down, a rainbow appeared. And God said, "I do set my rainbow in the cloud, and it shall be for a token of a covenant between me and the earth. And I will remember my covenant, which is between me and you and every living creature of all flesh; and the waters shall no more become a flood to destroy all flesh."*

So that's what rainbows are, Eric. And when you see one, enjoy its

---

* Genesis 9:13–15.

beauty, along with the fact that even though you are a wicked, evil little boy, great in your foulness and iniquity, the rainbow is a sign that God will not destroy all your flesh with water!

**Q:** *What happened to the dinosaurs?*—Susan Mosle, Asheville, North Carolina

**Mr. Science Guy:** Kids love dinosaurs, and with good reason. They're an intriguing part of our world's history. Dinosaurs were reptiles and they came in all shapes and sizes. Some were one hundred feet long, while others were as small as rabbits.

Even though they look like different animals, they were created at the same time; on the fifth day, to be exact. What happened was that God said let the earth bring forth the living creature after his kind, cattle, and creeping thing, and beast of the earth after his kind: and it was so. And God made the beast of the earth after his kind, and cattle after their kind, and every thing that creepeth upon the earth after his kind: and God saw that it was good.

The reason why the dinosaurs are gone is because of your ancient gender-mate Eve. God told her and Adam that they could eat the fruit of any tree of the garden, except a certain one, lest they die.

But Eve, being a woman, disobeyed God, and did partake of the fruit thereof, and then gave also unto her husband, and he did eat. This understandably made God very angry. He told Eve that he would greatly multiply her sorrow and her conception; and that Adam shall rule over her.

And, Susan, Eve did conceive, and man multiplied, but because of Eve's fall from grace, man continued to be evil. So, four thousand years ago, God destroyed every living thing with a flood, and the dinosaurs never came back. All because a woman disobeyed the word of the Lord Our God. Typical.

**Q:** *What is pi?*—Josh Dolan, Sioux Falls, South Dakota

**Mr. Science Guy:** Pi is a number that is mostly used in mathematical computations, and is written using the Greek letter for "p," π. Pi is the ratio of the circumference of any circle to the diameter of the same circle. No matter what the circle's size, this ratio will always equal pi. The letter π was first used for this number by William Jones in 1706.

Pi works out to roughly 3.14. But pi is an irrational number, which means that, in decimal form, the number never ends and never becomes repetitive.

This is in contrast to the number two, as in one man and one woman, which are the components of one marriage. This can be mathematically broken down as: 1 man + 1 woman = Marriage as God Has Defined It. That's why God said a man will leave his father and mother and be joined to his wife, and the two will become one flesh.

He didn't say a man and a man, Josh. Like you, Mr. Science Guy is only human. Like all men, he has sinned and fallen short in the eyes of God. We all have temptations, but God created Adam and Eve, Josh, not Adam and a guy he happened to meet in a gay bar one night after a speaking engagement at a church in Plano, Texas. That's the sort of thing that happens when you forget that a man shall not lie with another man as with a woman, for it is an abomination and they shall be put to death and their blood is upon them.

Luckily for Mr. Science Guy, and you, Josh, the Lord is compassionate and gracious, slow to anger, and abounding in loving kindness, and forgives iniquity, even a man lying with another man as with a woman and even if it was the only time that one of the men felt truly and completely happy.

**Q:** *What is global warming?*—Hanna Gottstein, St. Paul, Minnesota

**Mr. Science Guy:** Hanna, the short answer is this: a myth. Have you seen *Harry Potter and the Temple of Doom*? So-called global warming is about as real as that. In fact, they were both created by "Hollywood elites." The "global warming" doomsayers say that greenhouse gases, caused by humans, are increasing the world's temperatures, and that this will eventually cause all sorts of catastrophes.

Now, I see that you live in St. Paul, Hanna. Did you notice much "warming" there in Minnesota this past February? I bet you wish you did!

No, Hanna, global warming is a myth. All this talk about the temperature going up a tenth of a degree once every hundred years. Here's the science on what *is* going to happen.

The temperature will actually be going up, but not because of greenhouse gases. In fact, before that happens, it's going to get a lot colder. This is because of something called "the Tribulation." What will happen is that the sun shall be darkened, and the moon shall not give her light, and the stars shall fall from heaven, and the powers of the heavens shall be shaken: And then shall appear the sign of the Son of Man in heaven: and then shall all the tribes of the earth mourn, and they shall see the Son of Man coming in the clouds of heaven with power and great glory.

And the beast shall be taken, and with him the false prophet that wrought miracles before him, with which he deceived them that had received the mark of the beast, and them that worshipped his image. These shall both be cast alive into a lake of fire burning with brimstone.

There's your global warming. And that's science, not Hollywood make-'em-ups.

How can you prepare for this, you might be wondering, Hanna? Well, the first way—which might be a concern, judging from your name—is to not be Jewish, because they will lay their hands on you and will persecute you, delivering you to the synagogues and prisons, bringing you before kings and governors for His name's sake, and Jerusalem will be trampled under foot by the Gentiles until the times of the Gentiles are fulfilled.

I hope I've answered your question.

---

* Mr. Science Guy is an ordained minister who has nearly completed his BA in evangelism from Liberty University, and has sat in on courses at such colleges as the American Family Association Continuing Education Program and Focus on the Family's Internet Bible iCollege. He is currently doing a pre-doc fellowship at the First Baptist Church in Tyler, Texas.

# A WALK THROUGH HISTORY

So, in the new reality, what's going to become of culture? What about the symphony, independent film, libraries, six-dollar coffees, museums? Well, you won't have to give up all of those things. If you want to take your child for an educational field trip to the museum, you'll still be able to do that. Only you'll have to go to Cincinnati. We mean you'll *get* to go to Cincinnati.

It's called the Creation Museum. The $25-million, fifty-thousand-square-foot facility is set to open in 2007. According to the Web site of Answers in Genesis, the "Christian apologetics ministry" sponsoring this museum, its mission is to create "a wonderful alternative to the evolutionary natural history museums that are turning countless minds against the Gospel of Christ and the authority of the Scripture." The museum will be based on the "history book of the universe"—the Bible, which "pro-vides a reliable, eyewitness account of the beginning of all things."

Also from the Web site:

*1. Why is this museum needed?*

Our increasingly anti-Christian country must return to a belief in the authority of the Bible and be presented with the life-changing Gospel message. Evolutionary indoctrination has undermined the Christian foundations in America.

*2. What is so different about this museum?*

Almost all natural-history museums proclaim an evolution-ary, humanistic worldview. For example, they will typically place dinosaurs on an evolutionary timeline millions of years before man. AiG's museum will pro-claim the authority and accuracy of the Bible from Genesis to Rev-elation, and will show that there is a Creator, and that this Creator is Jesus Christ (Colossians 1:15–20), who is our Savior.

Answers in Genesis president Ken Ham told PBS that "the purpose of the Creation Museum is to equip Christians to have answers to defend their faith in today's world. Because let's face it, what's taught through the public schools and much of the secular media, it's really an attack on the Bible's history. It's really saying the Bible is not true. And many Christians just don't know how to handle those sorts of questions."*

To find out, Sam placed a call to the Creation Museum and asked a few of those sorts of questions:†

**Mark:** This is Mark. May I help you?

**Sam:** Hi Mark. It's Sam Seder calling from the *Majority Report*. I just wanted to find out what the Creation Museum was all about.

**Mark:** It's being built by Answers in Genesis. We're a Bible-defending organization. It will be a walk through history according to the Bible, but along the way we'll expose some of those grave problems with evolution theory.

**Sam:** So, for instance, carbon dating, you could look to the Bible for a solution, as opposed to the way scientists—

**Mark:** Evolutionists don't use carbon dating to date dinosaur fossils, for example.

**Sam:** What do they do?

**Mark:** Well, they use other dating methods, which have built-in assumptions and fudge factors and—

**Sam:** For example?

**Mark:** Well, at this point, I'd defer to one of the scientists who has a Ph.D.

**Sam:** I understand. So, what is the Christian version of why the

* "Evolution Debate," *Newshour with Jim Lehrer,* March 28, 2005.
† Edited for length and clarity.

dinosaurs aren't around anymore?

**Mark:** All right. Well, this is our model. This is our best guess. You know, you don't have scientific proof for the disappearance of dinosaurs. In fact, there are even some evolutionists today, one at the University of Chicago, who believe that there's a dinosaur even in Africa, today. We think that after a worldwide cataclysmic flood, the climate changed, less vegetation, people hunting dinosaurs, that they over the years started perishing—probably four thousand years ago. We have dragon legends around the world. We have the country flag of Wales that has a dragon on it. We have pictographs in Utah of dinosaur-like creatures. There's a lot of evidence that dinosaurs have been around recently.

*Proof that dinosaurs live among us: drawing by Jimmy Stevens, age 6.*

**Sam:** From your perspective, how old is the earth?

**Mark:** When the museum opens, we will take a position that the earth is . . . is young. It's certainly not millions or billions of years old.

**Sam:** Uh, between five and ten thousand years old?

**Mark:** Yes. We can't prove that. I mean, again, we are dealing with historical science as opposed to observational science.

**Sam:** When did humans show up?

**Mark:** Just after the dinosaurs. The sixth day of creation. That's our belief. We believe the best facts of science, when best interpreted, support that dinosaurs and humans have been contemporaneous.

So there you have it. That's how we began—the sixth day. Pretty simple. And our ending—just as simple . . .

# 4 · APOCALYPSE NOW

So when does all this end, you're thinking. Surely, this can't go on forever. Well, you're in luck. The good news is that there will be an actual ending. The bad news is, it will likely end with you spending all of eternity in a lake of fire.

It's called the Apocalypse, also known as "the end times," "millennialism," and "eschatology," though you shouldn't use that last word; it will be taken as a sign that you're an intellectual, which they'll take to mean that you don't believe in it. That won't fare you so well when it all "goes down."

But it's not really going to happen, right? I mean, isn't that all just a bunch of mumbo jumbo?

Maybe. Maybe not. It's not just the Rapture Right that believes it's going to happen. So does your president. And when the president of the United States believes something is going to happen, well, it usually happens.

Among evangelical Christians, 89 percent believe that every word in the Bible is literally true. Yes, that's just evangelical Christians. But in 1984, 24 percent of the country called themselves evangelical Christians. In 2003, that number was up to 30 percent. At the current rates of expansion, and according to the mathematical model we've formulated,* by the year 2145 the entire country—100 percent of us—will be evangelical Christians.

Among Republicans, the number who say they believe in the literal truth of the Bible is already up to 77 percent. Why the discrepancy between the numbers for Republicans and evangelicals? Aren't they the same thing? The only explanation we can find for this gap is that many of the closeted homosexual Republicans probably answered "no" out of sheer hope.

Among those in the Bush administration, the number is probably even higher. Bush's first attorney general, John Ashcroft, is certainly a true believer. According to his memoir, when taking the oath of office at various points in his career, he would—like the "ancient kings of Israel"—have himself anointed with oil. Cooking oil, to be exact. When assuming the office of senator from Missouri, he used Crisco.† No word on whether he has switched to one of the newer, more trendy anointments, like canola oil, which has no trans-fatty acids. When Ashcroft was sworn in as attorney general, Justice Clarence Thomas was the chosen one to lube him on up.‡, §

But the holy oil isn't just limited to the executive branch. In January 2005, in the week leading up to the confirmation hearings for Justice Samuel Alito, three evangelical ministers claimed to have snuck into the Judiciary Committee room where the hearings would be held and

---

* Full disclosure: Stephen has a degree in history, Sam spent a year in law school. Though in sixth grade Sam described math as "my favorite subject."

† From Ashcroft's autobiography *Lessons from a Father to His Son* (Thomas Nelson Publishers, 1998).

‡ We note that the memoir of Gore campaign manager Donna Brazil is called *Cooking with Grease*. We're not sure what significance this has, but it's pretty freaky.

§ For the sake of fairness, Sam concedes that he is "addicted" to his "olive-oil mister." He sprays olive oil on everything, from corn on the cob to his baby's butt.

"anointed" the senators' seats with oil.* "We did adequately apply oil to all the seats," said Reverend Rob Schenk, dispelling concerns that they had perhaps used only a light "anointing-oil mister." They also claimed to have done it for John Roberts. Did it work? They both got confirmed.

And then there's Bush himself. After waking up on his fortieth birthday with a hangover, he decided to quit drinking. His inspiration was a visit by Reverend Billy Graham to the Bush compound in Kennebunkport. According to Bush, in his memoir *A Charge to Keep*:

> I don't remember the exact words. It was more the power of his example. The Lord was so clearly reflected in his gentle and loving demeanor. The next day . . . Graham planted a mustard seed in my soul . . . he led me to the path, and I began walking. And it was the beginning of a change in my life. I had always been a religious person, had regularly attended church, even taught Sunday school and served as an altar boy. But that weekend my faith took on a new meaning. It was the beginning of a new walk where I would recommit my heart to Jesus Christ.†

Around that same time, he began going to the Midland Men's Community Bible Study Group.

In 1993, in an interview in the *Houston Chronicle*, Bush said that, in the words of the reporter, "heaven is open only to those who accept Jesus Christ."

Seven years later, in his first presidential campaign, Bush was asked in a Republican primary debate to name his favorite philosopher. His reply: "Christ."

Though it's well known the Holy Spirit is the brains behind the whole Trinity Operation, and Bush doesn't seem to pay much attention to some parts of his Best Friend Forever's actual philosophy—stuff like "Sell all

---

* "Ministers Say They Blessed Seats Ahead of Alito Hearing," June Kronholz, *Wall Street Journal*, January 5, 2006.
† With that said, reports are that Bush has started drinking "near beer."

that you have, and give to the poor"*—the point is, there's a pretty good chance that, as they say, the end is nigh. Or at least nighish.

And you can monitor it right on your computer. Raptureready.com is a Web site that says it has two functions:

1) To factor together a number of related end time components into a cohesive indicator

2) To standardize those components to eliminate the wide variance that currently exists with prophecy reporting.

It's no secret that prophecy reporting has gotten completely out of hand lately. So Raptureready.com aims to reform it by taking a constant analysis of forty-five factors. The variables include:

> False Christs
> Satanism
> Leadership
> Beast Government
> Gog (Russia)
> Global Turmoil
> Wild Weather
> Oil Supply/Price
> Supernatural
> Mark of the Beast
> Inflation
> Kings of the East
> Liberalism
> Tribulation Temple

Each item is assigned a number, most of which seem to range from one to five, the total of which is the Rapture Index. Right now, the index sits at

---

* Mark 10:21.

160. This is nearly the highest it's been in two years (the record is 182, on September 24, 2001).

What's been going on lately? Well, the "Floods" category got a boost from Katrina: "Hurricane Katrina has upgraded this category." Also, "Plagues," "Drought," "Famine" have been getting some good action. Katrina also gave a boost to the "Leadership" total: "Hurricane Katrina has cause [sic] a surge in end-time active [sic]."

We're not sure what that means, but we're pretty sure it's not good.

There are other signs, too. John Bolton, for instance. He is thought by many to be the Antichrist, and some experts believe his mustache may be the mark of the Beast.

## THE FOUR MUSTACHES OF THE APOCALYPSE

Some say the mark of the Beast is the mustache of John Bolton. Others say it's that of the *New York Times*'s Thomas Friedman. (Though a provocative new theory asserts that the two mustaches are actually the same mustache.) In any case, theologians are pretty sure the Beast will have some sort of facial hair, and they've narrowed it down to four possibilities. Can you guess which of the following mustaches belong to which man?

1          2          3          4

A) John Bolton
B) Thomas Friedman
C) Saddam Hussein
D) David Crosby

Also, Trent Lott, whose house on the Gulf was washed away in Hurricane Katrina, sings in a barbershop quartet, a kind of music that many believe is what the Four Horsemen of the Apocalypse would sound like were they to sing in harmony and wear suspenders and straw hats.

What does the total number mean? The Web site includes a handy index to the index:

**Rapture index of 110 to 145: Heavy prophetic activity**

**Rapture index above 145: Fasten your seat belts**

Let us remind you again, we're at 160.

The site also includes an Armageddon Clock, because ". . . a group of scientists developed a Doomsday clock to measure the peril of nuclear war. Because events of the tribulation poses [sic] an even greater danger to earth inhabitants, we decided to create an Armageddon Clock to provide a point of reference."

The clock begins in the "1800s," in which it was "30 minutes to midnight." As of 2004 (the clock needs servicing, apparently), it is "3 minutes to midnight."

That's it. The Apocalypse, as they say, "is on." The ending is beginning.

So what's going to happen to you? Will it be fun? Do you need reservations? Will you have to share a bathroom? Will it affect your decisions about a mortgage, and, if so, should you go fixed-rate or variable?

Welcome to:

## THE F.U.B.A.R. GUIDE TO YOUR PLACE IN THE APOCALYPSE

*What is the Apocalypse?*

The Apocalypse, also known as Armageddon, or the End of the World, is the final battle between the kings of the earth, representing Satan and led by Satan's top lieutenant and former lawyer for the International Arab Horse Association, the Antichrist,* and God's armies, led by Jesus, and just because he is God's son in no way means he wasn't the most qualified

---

* Actually he was just the Judges and Stewards commissioner.

for the job (unlike his biggest fan in the whole wide world, Jesus was actually the smart brother). The entire thing is chronicled in the last book of the New Testament, the Book of Revelations.

*When is all this going to happen?*
Our calculations show that the Apocalypse will begin shortly after sales of this book begin to slip. Either that, or when Kevin Federline gets his own reality show.*

*Will the Apocalypse necessarily involve me?*
Probably. It's going to be pretty hard to escape. Think of it sort of like the ultimate television reality show, one in which the entire universe made the cut, and not just the usual personal trainers.

*What happens to the winners and losers?*
The winners get to live with God in "a new heaven and a new earth" forever, and receive an exclusive record contract with Simon Cowell and Atlantic Records. The losers will die in one of a variety of ways—earthquakes, locusts, plagues, famine, pestilence, fire coming down from the sky. After which they will spend eternity in a burning lake of fire with Satan.

*A new heaven and a new earth sound better to me than a burning lake of fire. Is there anything I can do to prepare?*
Your best bet here is to convert and become a fundamentalist Christian. But the fact that you're even reading this is not a good sign.

*I'm an atheist. How does it look for me?*
Not good. On the plus side, the fact that you're an atheist probably means you're not a member of Satan's army. If you don't get killed in the first round of wars and plagues, you might make it to the Rapture, the episode

---

* "Britney Spears and her husband Kevin Federline are to star in their own reality TV show, it has been revealed." *BBC News,* April 5, 2005. Oh. My. God.

in which Jesus returns and takes all the Christians with him. If you make it through this, there will be some good real estate deals to be had, particularly in the South. After this, it's to the burning lake of fire for you.

*Well, I'm a Jew, surely this means I can "opt out."*
Sorry, even worse for you than the atheist. But on the other hand, you do play a critical role in the Apocalypse, though sort of the way bayonet dummies play a critical role in basic training.

Since it was necessary that Israel exist again before the Apocalypse could start, many Rapture Right Christians are big fans of Israel. For now. Israel needs to stick around at least long enough to rebuild the Temple. After that, well, Israel will have played its part.

In fact, according to Republican presidential candidate and amateur meteorologist Pat Robertson, "the Antichrist is probably a Jew alive in Israel today."* In fact, so vigilant is the reverend about Israel, and so attuned to God, that he alone knew what it was that really struck Prime Minister Ariel Sharon down:

> I think we need to look at the Bible and the Book of Joel. The prophet Joel makes it very clear that God has enmity against those who, quote, "divide my land." God considers this land to be his. You read the Bible, he says, "This is my land." And for any prime minister of Israel who decides he is going carve it up and give it away, God says, "No. This is mine" . . . [Sharon] was dividing God's land, and I would say woe unto any prime minister of Israel who takes a similar course to appease the EU, the United Nations or United States of America. God said, "This land belongs to me, you better leave it alone."†

---

* Attributed to him in the *Harper's Magazine* article "The Christian Paradox: How a Faithful Nation Gets Jesus Wrong," Bill McKibben, August, 2005. And in fairness to the reverend, he only said "probably."

† Said on his program *The 700 Club*, January 5, 2006. Transcript via Media Matters, at http://mediamatters.org/items/200601050004.

We'd like to think that at least Pat was saying that it was *Sharon's* God that struck him down, in which case the statement would have an ecumenical element, but that may be giving him too much credit. In any case, if being Jewish isn't going to save Ariel Sharon, it's not looking good for you.

But there is a bright spot. If you're lucky enough to make it all the way until the seventh seal (and the others are all pretty bad, like the sixth: ". . . a great earthquake. The sun turned black like sackcloth made of goat hair, the whole moon turned blood red, and the stars in the sky fell to earth, as late figs drop from a fig tree when shaken by a strong wind"—Revelations 6:12), you might just have a chance. Right before the seventh seal is broken, 144,000 Jews—12,000 from each of the twelve tribes—are "sealed" by an angel. We're not exactly sure what this means, but it could mean that these Jews, unlike all the others, are "saved." But only if they convert.

*I'm a homosexual . . .*
You're doomed. Really, really doomed.

*I'm a Democrat.*
Satan. Fire. Lake. Eternity.

# 5 · THE NEW AMERICAN DREAM

Ah, the American Dream, you work hard, play by the rules, you get rich, get a nice house, your kids go to college and do better than you.

Savor those memories. Because those days are gone. That particular dream had a nice run, but the expiration date on it just passed. But don't despair. It's been replaced by a new American dream. And this one's a lot simpler.

We've distilled each of them into a handy chart that should show you the difference:

**Old American Dream: get rich.**

**New American Dream: be rich.**

You see? Richness is still involved, still a key component, still all up in there. And all those things that you could acquire if you worked hard enough under the old American Dream are still there. The difference is, if you don't already have them, you're unlikely to get them. But if you do have them, congratulations!

Remember when Hurricane Katrina was blowing through, and everyone realized that poor people existed when the media made poverty the
new Hilton sisters? You just got a glimpse of your future, only without
that foxy Anderson Cooper.

The American Dream had the roof blown off by Hurricane Bush,* and
now it's been "reconstructed" (with no-bid contracts) into the New American Dream. The ladder that was at the heart of the old American Dream
has been replaced by a slide, a really slippery slide. You can still try to go
up. But you're more likely to go down.

Rapture Rightists aren't the only type of fundamentalists in the Republican Party. There's also the market fundamentalists. They're not religious,
but they're just as faith-based. Show a market fundie that Medicare is far
more efficient and cost-effective than private health insurance† and his
response is, "We need even more privatization."

The market fundamentalists view their religious partners as lunatics,
but useful lunatics. Michael Scanlon, a former aide to Tom DeLay and Jack
Abramoff's partner, who pled guilty in November 2005 to conspiracy to
bribe public officials, laid it out in a memo he sent to an Indian tribe about
the strategy he would use on their behalf:

> The wackos get their information through the Christian right, Chris-
> tian radio, mail, the internet and telephone trees . . . Simply put, we
> want to bring out the wackos to vote *against* something and make sure
> the rest of the public lets the whole thing slip past them.‡

The religious fundamentalists agree to overlook that all the money

---

* After the 2004 election, he was upgraded from a Cat. 4 to a Cat. 5.
† Administrative costs for Medicare are 3 percent, versus almost 13 percent for private insurance.
The Commonwealth Fund, March 10, 2003, paper: "Time for Change: The Hidden Cost of a Frag-
mented Health Insurance System."
‡ "Abramoff-Scanlon School of Sleaze," Michael Scherer, *Salon,* November 3, 2005.

being made by the market guys comes from less-than-Jesus-like endeavors, because their organizations get a lot of funding from the market fundamentalists.*

It all comes together in something called the "Ownership Society." Which is another way of saying "Society for the Owners." A society where the owners of capital (you know, the stuff whose "gains" are now taxed at a reduced rate, or not at all, like second houses, stocks, bonds, trusts, et cetera) accrue money faster and with less taxation. A society where the nonowners—wackos who make their living from working and "paychecks"—carry the full burden.

So here you have the New American Dream. It's even better than the old one, because it leaves less to chance. If you've got the cash, it's a lot easier now to . . . get more cash.

If not, the good news is that you're still perfectly free to dream about the Old American Dream. And nobody can take that away.

---

* Over two billion dollars in faith-based initiative dollars in 2004. "Bush: faith-based initiative still has a prayer," Bill Straub, Scripps Howard News Service, March 1, 2005.

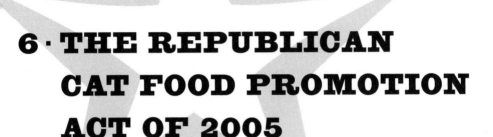

# 6 · THE REPUBLICAN CAT FOOD PROMOTION ACT OF 2005

The Bush Social Security Plan. It just won't die. Like a horror-movie villain—every time those crazy teens camping out in the strangely isolated woods think they're finally safe and go back to drinking and dancing around in their underwear, he suddenly breaks through the window or kills the guy who went out to get more beer.

Bush's plan might look a bit different each time he rolls it out, but at the end of the day, its purpose will still be to kill the most successful government program in our nation's history.

This is why Democrats defend it. This is also why Republicans attack it: take down Social Security, and you've basically taken down the entire idea of government. It is to the market fundamentalists what evolution is to the religious side. But it's proving harder than they thought.

Social Security's real name is Old-Age, Survivors, and Disability Insurance (OASDI). Its purpose is to insure workers and families against the loss of income due to not just retirement but also disability and death.

How effective is it? Right now it's keeping 13 million people out of poverty. It represents 60 percent of the income of the average sixty-five-year-old. Take away Social Security, and one of every two elderly people is in poverty. With Social Security, the rate falls to one in twelve. For around a third of the elderly, Social Security provides their entire income.

What doesn't it do? Well, it doesn't provide a big year-end bonus for Wall Street brokers, it doesn't artificially inflate the value of the stock market, it doesn't allow for a one-time $2 trillion upward redistribution of wealth to the already wealthy. Finally, it doesn't provide the shot in the arm to the cat-food industry, which privatization would.

Republicans have wanted to destroy Social Security since the day it was instituted on August 14, 1935. Before FDR could even sign it, almost every Republican in the House voted to kill it by sending it back to committee. The 1936 GOP nominee, Alf Landon, called it "unjust, unworkable, stupidly drafted, and wastefully financed." Three years later, when Social Security benefits were extended to survivors, again, three-quarters of the Republicans voted against it. In 1950, Social Security was extended to the disabled, which drew nay votes from 89 percent of the Republicans. In 1964, Barry Goldwater openly campaigned for its elimination.

Bush, however, came up with a new murder weapon. It would be disguised as nothing less than an attempt to "save" Social Security. He would, in effect, love it to death.

The following is from an e-mail written by Peter H. Wehner, Karl Rove's deputy. It was made public in January of 2005.

> Let me tell you first what our plans are in terms of sequencing and political strategy. We will focus on Social Security immediately in this new year. Your strategy will probably include speeches early this month to establish an important premise: the current system is heading for an iceberg. The notion that younger workers will receive anything like the benefits they have been promised is fiction, unless significant reforms are undertaken. We need to establish in the public mind a key fiscal fact: right now we are on an unsustainable course. That reality

needs to be seared into the public consciousness; it is the pre-condition
to authentic reform.

In order to kill this thing they've been hostile to for a long time, they
need political cover. So first they need to whip up an aura of crisis, a sense
of what you might call an . . . imminent threat. Wehner later admits the
real reason:

> For the first time in six decades, the Social Security battle is one we can
> win—and in doing so, we can help transform the political and philo-
> sophical landscape of the country.

In fact, there is a crisis: Medicare. But this one is real, and it doesn't lend
itself so well to the philosophical landscape-changing possibilities that
Social Security does.

Bush's plan differed from the other clumsy Republican attempts over
the past six decades to kill Social Security by being a two-part assault. First,
diagnose a problem in Social Security, then kill it with the medicine—the
so-called private accounts.

The first murder attempt, launched in the spring of 2005, failed. And,
oddly enough, it was because of the media. After all, the same MO had
worked in Iraq. But, it turns out, it was a lot easier and safer for journalists
and bloggers to go down to the Congressional Budget Office and pick up
details on Social Security's health than it was to zip over to Iraq to find out
whether Saddam had "nuclear weapon–related programs."

What they found was that there was no crisis. It wouldn't be until 2017
that Social Security would need to use the interest being earned on the
trust fund. And not until 2027 would it need the trust-fund assets themselves. And not until 2053 would Social Security begin to need general
funds. And that's all if absolutely nothing is done, and assuming fairly
pessimistic numbers.

So that's the "crisis." What about Bush's "cure"? Even Bush finally
had to admit that privatized accounts would actually make Social Security
less solvent. And they would do it much quicker. Right off the bat,

privatization would require a transition cost of $2.2 trillion. Had Bush really wanted to improve the health of Social Security, he might have taken something away from this fact:

> **Ratio of Bush's tax cuts to the Social Security shortfall over the next seventy-five years: three to one.\***

Oh, also, we're not supposed to say "privatization." Bush switched to the more palatable "personal accounts." These wouldn't be sold as a cure for Social Security—just a "better deal."

Well, that turns out not to be true, either. Though the Republicans like to think—and want you to think—of Social Security as a "welfare" program, it's actually an insurance program. Just as you pay car insurance to ensure that you won't go destitute if you get into a car accident, you pay into Social Security to ensure that, if you don't have wads of cash when you retire, you won't be forced to eat cat food.

Think of it like this: does it bum you out when you don't get into a car wreck, because of all the car insurance you've paid for? For most of us, it's useful to know that, if we're a wreck by the time we retire, there will be something waiting there to keep us out of poverty.

That's why Social Security is known as a guaranteed benefit plan. Bush's private—we mean "personal"—accounts are what is known as a guaranteed contribution plan. You are guaranteed to pay into the plan, but you are guaranteed nothing as far as what will come out. In trying to draw a parallel here, the only pithy example that comes to mind is roulette (though all gambling suffices). You have to lay down a bet, but you don't have to get anything back. So why does Bush say this is a better deal?

Bush tries to sell private accounts because they offer a higher rate of return than Social Security. Which, sadly, is also untrue.

---

\* "Administration's Tax Cuts Worsen Prospects for Bridging 75-Year Gap in Social Security and Medicare," Robert Greenstein, Center on Budget and Policy Priorities, March 19, 2003.

## BUSH AND SOCIAL SECURITY: IT'S NOT ALL LIES

We realize hearing about all the Republican lies can get discouraging. It's no fun to realize that virtually everything the president says about something is false. So, to keep your morale up, and to be fair to President Bush, here's a list of things that are true about Bush's statements and understanding of Social Security:

★ Social Security does exist.

★ The years 2015, 2042, and 2053 are in the future and will, at some point, arrive.

★ There are such things as "accounts" and "the elderly."

★ The word "crisis" is a real word, and some things (just not Social Security) are, in fact, in crisis.

★ People do age and people do retire.

★ Time is linear.

We've all heard the line "over the course of forty years the stock market pays a 7 percent return on your money." But, of course, it depends on which forty years. Not to mention, that 7 percent number? That's an average—some people will do much better, some people will do much worse.

But here's the worst part—and this is the part that Bush doesn't talk about too much—his "private accounts" are just loans. And that's because of something called the "clawback." This was the device that would allow Bush to hide the proposed benefit cuts necessary under privatization.

Right now, we all pay 6.2 percent of the first $90,000 we make into Social Security. Bush wants you to divert two-thirds of that into your private accounts. Now Bush wants you to believe that when you hit retirement age, you'll get all that money back, plus the "magic of compound interest."

But the four percentage points you've "diverted" into private accounts is not your money—it was all just a loan from the government. And when you retire, you will pay all of that money back to the government—they will "claw it back," if you will (and, under Bush's plan, you will). The great news is that you get to keep all that's left over—minus, of course, 3 percent interest above the rate of inflation.

Not to worry—if you are one of the lucky few who did extraordinarily well in the stock market, you may have actually made slightly more than you would have under the old Social Security system. But that's not too likely. If you don't have phenomenal luck, you're basically screwed—because you still owe the government their "clawback." And guess where that comes from? The two percentage points of your money—the only money remaining for you—that stayed in the guaranteed benefit system. Enjoy your cat food—if you can afford it.

The last boon for the cat-food industry in the plan is something called the "inflation indexing." Right now, Social Security benefits are paid out each year according to a "wage index." The "inflation index" will always give you fewer benefits. Bush likes to use the term "inflation index" instead of "benefit cut," because "inflation index" makes you sleepy and "benefit cut" tends to alarm people.

What kind of cuts are we talking about? The cuts would affect 70 percent of all workers. For someone who is thirty-five in the year 2002, the average cut would be 17 percent. For someone who is twenty-five in 2002, it would be 25 percent. For someone retiring in 2075, it would be 46 percent. That is, if the clawback leaves you with any money at all.

Remember how we all made fun of Al Gore when he said "lockbox"? We do. We remember saying to people, "Why does he keep saying 'lockbox' so much? It makes him sound like a douche bag." Turns out, we're the douche bags. If Gore, or anybody else, for that matter, had been able to put a lock on that box, Bush wouldn't be able to sneak in and grab the trust fund and spend it somewhere else (hey, you guys—more tax cuts!).

Well, actually, Bush doesn't need tax cuts for the wealthy in this case, because the Social Security setup already benefits them (and even this isn't enough). That's because only the first $90,000 a person makes in payroll income (as opposed to interest on your bank account, or capital gains from selling your house in Aspen or selling a building) is taxed for Social Security. So the Social Security Trust Fund is made up of tax dollars from workers and wage earners.

In 1983, Social Security taxes were raised to create the trust fund to better withstand demographic shifts when an increased number of people retire relative to the number of people still working. The bad news is we are about to hit one of those periods as the baby boomers retire. The good news is raising the Social Security taxes worked and created a huge surplus in the trust fund. The bad news is Al Gore never got his lock for the box, and George Bush has already raided the trust fund for tax cuts.

In addition to just the sheer joy of giving wealthy people more money, one of the effects of the tax cuts—and one, no doubt, in the minds of Bush and Rove—was that bleeding the Treasury would help foment the sense of crisis they needed to destroy Social Security. It's not like they wouldn't have done it had they known Social Security would be in jeopardy. It was done partly specifically to throw Social Security into a crisis—or at least make it easier to make the case for the crisis. It would be pretty hard to gin up the fear if we were still sitting on the $5.6 trillion projected surplus with which Bush came into office. He had to get rid of it. And the wealthy were generous enough to take it off his hands.

# 7 · SENIOR CITIZEN CAREER-COUNSELING GUIDE

Okay, so at some point Bush is probably going to succeed in screwing up Social Security. And if he does, what then? We've got you covered. This section is for retirees, senior citizens, and those approaching retirement. And even if you're not in those groups, it still contains valuable information for you. With any luck, at some point you're going to be a senior citizen, unless, of course, the Rapture happens, in which case, given that you're reading this book, you're most likely going to spend eternity in all-consuming hellfire and damnation. But, hey, we'll be there, too—and we'll refund you the prorated amount for reading this chapter.

That said, welcome to the Senior Citizen Career-counseling Guide. Unless you're one of the lucky few who happen to be independently wealthy or had the foresight to invest in the booming Rapture-tech sector stocks, the retirement landscape for you is mixed.

Yeah, sure, there's still probably going to be some system called something like "Social Security." It's not going to help you, however. That money hasn't disappeared—it's just been given to people other than you. People like Wall Street investment bankers and financial services executives. The good news is that all your money is being invested and strategically used to create even more wealth. The bad news is that the wealth your money is creating is other people's wealth. There is a chance, though, that if you write to some of the people who *do* have your money, they might tell you what they're doing with it, maybe even send you a photo of the yacht or third house you helped them buy, but that's about the only interaction you're going to have with that money ever again.

"What about my pension?" Ah, that's cute. Those are quickly disappearing. Over the past decade, half of all pension plans have disappeared. United Airlines bailed out of its plan in the summer of 2005; in December, Verizon announced it was ending defined-benefit pensions for fifty thousand management employees; and in January of 2006, IBM, a perfectly healthy company, announced that it was freezing its employee pension plan. Once this starts spreading, and it already has, every business will feel it has to do the same to stay competitive. So, say good-bye to the pension.

"But wait, what am I going to live on? I was counting on that money. Do I have any options?" Of course you do. You have a great option. It's called the United States labor market. There are literally tens of millions of jobs out there. It's just a matter of finding the right one.

"Hold on, you mean after busting my hump for forty years, being a hardworking American, paying my taxes, I'm going to have to work until I die?" Yes, that's what we mean.

But just because you're old, tired, in frail health, and in the early stages of senility doesn't mean you can't find a satisfying job with which to begin your second, or third, or whatever—let's just call it final—career.

Yes, to some, the thought of returning to work after retirement, or continuing to work after you believed you were going to retire, is not a happy one. Well, that's job one right there: changing that bad attitude. Look at it this way: this whole thing can be a blessing. The news is full of stories about retirees who couldn't adjust to the change of routine or who weren't surrounded by a supportive social network and became isolated. That's not so good for your health, either. You know what solves that problem? That's right: a job. In fact, there's already a term for it: "work-related retirement."

Say it enough times, and the contradiction starts to wear off. Sort of like "illness-related cure," or "peace-related war," or "Rumsfeld-related honesty."

Or think of it this way: you're simply picking a new hobby—one that you're going to be *paid for*, even perhaps just above minimum wage. How many people get paid to enjoy their hobbies—and then get to enjoy them forty, fifty, even sixty hours a week?

Now you're coming around.

\* \* \*

## PICKING THE JOB THAT'S RIGHT FOR ME

Naturally, job hunting at your age poses some unique challenges. Some of you may be thinking, I'm old, I can't do most jobs, most employers are going to want someone younger. And you'd be right. And while the job market for you now is certainly more limited than it was when you were younger, there is still an infinite variety of jobs out there. We're here to help you find the job you'll enjoy and find most fulfilling—or (whom are we kidding?) at least not hate that much and find the least soul-crushing. Wise career planning requires making informed decisions. Here are some tools that will help you through this process:

*Define the problem.*
Your problem is that you're old and tired and sick of working, and you just want to rest a little and enjoy the years you have left before you die, but you can't do this, because you have no money to retire with.

*Define your long-term goal.*
Not starving or freezing to death.

*Define your short-term goal that will help you accomplish your long-term goal.*
Your short-term goal is to find a job that you're able to do and that will pay you enough so you won't starve or freeze to death.

*Take action.*

Get out there, swallow your pride, and ask the seventeen-year-old at the counter for a job application. Use your hunger—it's one of your best, and only, tools.

## THE SCIENTIFIC SENIOR CITIZEN CAREER-COUNSELING QUIZ

The following is a handy quiz that will assist you in identifying your skills, abilities, and interests. It takes only a few minutes, which is good, because time is not exactly on your side.

| | DISAGREE STRONGLY | DISAGREE SOMEWHAT | UNSURE | AGREE SOMEWHAT | AGREE STRONGLY |
|---|---|---|---|---|---|
| I like working with people. | ☐ | ☐ | ☐ | ☐ | ☐ |
| I am very organized. | ☐ | ☐ | ☐ | ☐ | ☐ |
| I can stand up. | ☐ | ☐ | ☐ | ☐ | ☐ |
| I can still drive a car. | ☐ | ☐ | ☐ | ☐ | ☐ |
| Being yelled at by a teenager does not bother me. | ☐ | ☐ | ☐ | ☐ | ☐ |
| I know my name. | ☐ | ☐ | ☐ | ☐ | ☐ |
| I am willing to take strong psychopharmacological drugs. | ☐ | ☐ | ☐ | ☐ | ☐ |
| I am not litigious. | ☐ | ☐ | ☐ | ☐ | ☐ |
| I am not given to crying uncontrollably when I think of my life. | ☐ | ☐ | ☐ | ☐ | ☐ |
| I am continent. | ☐ | ☐ | ☐ | ☐ | ☐ |
| I am willing to wear an animal costume. | ☐ | ☐ | ☐ | ☐ | ☐ |
| I don't sunburn easily. | ☐ | ☐ | ☐ | ☐ | ☐ |
| I am not given to sudden rages, or, if I am, I do not own any semiautomatic firearms. | ☐ | ☐ | ☐ | ☐ | ☐ |
| I can work a deep fryer. | ☐ | ☐ | ☐ | ☐ | ☐ |
| I'm not one to always be going on about the need for "more breaks," or "overtime pay," or "working toilets." | ☐ | ☐ | ☐ | ☐ | ☐ |

I like the smell of livestock. ☐ ☐ ☐ ☐ ☐
I realize that playful nicknames like "Pops,"
    "Grandma," "Methuselah," "Ol' Lady," "Corpsy,"
    "Mrs. Cadaver" are just harmless workplace fun. ☐ ☐ ☐ ☐ ☐
I am not afraid of rats or large vermin. ☐ ☐ ☐ ☐ ☐
I'm not a stickler about workplace safety laws. ☐ ☐ ☐ ☐ ☐
I am willing to enlist in a combat unit. ☐ ☐ ☐ ☐ ☐

Congratulations! You've completed the F.U.B.A.R. Scientific Senior Citizen Career-counseling Quiz. To get your results, and determine which job is right for you, simply give yourself 1 point for each "disagree strongly," 2 for "disagree somewhat," 3 for "unsure," 4 for "agree somewhat," and 5 for "agree strongly."

Now add up your score. Here's the answer key:

If your score was 0–100 points, the best jobs for you are:

1) minimum-wage job
2) below-minimum-wage job

★ ★ ★

## OVERVIEW

There, that wasn't so hard, was it? Now at least you know what you're looking at for your golden years, and can narrow down your options—and dreams, hopes, and the years themselves—accordingly. And do you find the ins and outs of health care plans—all that HMO, PPO, HPO, copay, deductible gobbledygook—difficult to follow? Well, that's great, because in your new job, you won't have to know any of that. Put all that gibber-gabbish out of your mind.

Yes, there are lots of minimum-wage and below-minimum-wage jobs. But which are best for me, you're wondering? The short answer: any of them you can get.

But, more specifically, given your unique skill set, you might find it's worth targeting some more than others.

Here are some jobs we've determined make the most of your special needs and abilities:

> migrant farmworker
> medical experiment subject
> porn booth clerk

Of course, this isn't the entire list of the jobs available to you—this is just a tool to help you achieve the best retirement possible. There's also Chicken Shack leaflet distribution person.

This, then, *is* the entire list of jobs available to you. So buck up, get out there, and get started on your not-so-golden years. With any luck, you'll die soon.

# 8 · FUN THINGS TO DO WHEN YOU'RE BROKE

Poverty. It's got such a negative sound to it. It's all about what you don't have. But for the vast majority of us who aren't going to be the "owners" in the new "ownership society," we'd better get used to it.

Not everybody, of course. Not, for instance, the people in Bush's original cabinet, whose average wealth was around $11 million. Or for the top 1 percent, who own 40 percent of the nation's wealth. But you're probably not one of those (if you are, however, *F.U.B.A.R.* is available for bulk sales, and makes great Christmas—or severance—gifts for your employees, domestics, indentured servants, and underlings). But more for the rest of us, those affected by facts like:

★ Real hourly wages have fallen 2.2 percent since the tax cut in 2003

★ Median household income has dropped every year Bush has been president

★ The poverty rate has risen each year since 2001

★ In the thirty-month period after the end of the recession, the economy has added 4.5 million jobs, compared with 7.9 million in the corresponding period following the last three recessions

★ As of August 2005, the personal savings rate has dropped to –2.18 percent, the lowest rate since the Great Depression

★ The average American pays nearly 14 percent of disposable income just to pay off personal debt

So, that's it, a lot of you are gonna be poor. On the plus side, with the old American Dream, there were all those different levels, all that striving, all that wondering whether you were going to "make it," all those mortgage details, college application forms, decisions about schools for your children. Now, no more worrying about "keeping up with the Joneses." They're poor, too!

The New American Dream is so much easier. It's like using the 1040 EZ form instead of itemizing. Only easier. You just put "zero" in all the boxes. And you're done. Think of all the time you'll save. Always wanted to write that novel? What about that idea you once had about learning Portuguese? Or that plan you had that one time to really—I'm serious this time—learn about wine? Of course, those are just metaphors; those actually do require some money and you won't have any of that, but you get the idea.

The point is, your new life of soul-crushing poverty doesn't mean you can't have fun. The dark, grim Dickensian notions of poverty are over. In the New America, it'll be hip to be poor. You heard it here first: Poverty is the new black. So forget about all those stress-inducing, time-consuming chores like planning "vacation," and traveling, and having to log on to sites like Expedia, and Travelocity, and Amazon, and remembering your passwords, and making all those choices about what to buy, where to go, is my billing address the same as my shipping address blah blah blah blah blah. Those are all in your past. Your future is much simpler.

Don't believe us? Here are just a few ways to spice up your life under the New American Dream, and have fun without having money:

*Daydreaming*

An old, simple pleasure, now back again. You just sit somewhere—or, if you can't afford a chair, you can even do this one standing—and think about things. Think about your life, think about how you used to travel, how you used to own stuff, how when you were hungry, you'd buy something and then eat it.

And the cost? Absolutely free, at least financially. Depending on psychological makeup, some will want to steer clear of using their own life as daydreaming fodder.

For those who might find such daydreaming worrisome, or those (like the vast majority of the country) without health insurance, here are some other, perhaps less fraught daydreaming building-blocks you can use. Of course, you're free to come up with your own, these are just suggestions:

The sun sure is bright. Why is it so bright?

Why can a bird fly, but a fly can't bird?

What are the dreams of blind people like?

What's the deal with Ashton Kutcher?

Why is "abbreviation" such a long word?

Why don't sheep shrink when it rains?

*Be a Good Person* and *Get High*

Yeah, those were the days. Buy some drugs, get high, forget your problems for a while. The problem is, that costs money. And now that you don't have any, you want to get high even more. Here's a quick solution that not only works but will leave you feeling a little better about yourself.

It's called selling your blood, or, more accurately, selling a lot of your blood. There is a little bit of cost involved—in the form of fake IDs. This is because, technically, you're only supposed to donate blood every eight weeks. And with all the testing that they do, you can't just give them a fake name. So the better your fake ID is, the easier this is going to be.

Once you've got your "documentation" on you, we've found that donating blood about once every five days or so is enough to keep you feeling permanently "high."

And the beauty part is that every time you go, they give you free snacks: cookies, chocolate, a piece of fruit.

It's a win-win for your new life as a loser in the New America.

### Divorce

Make a game out of your marriage dissolving. We all know the strain that financial difficulties put on a marriage. And, yes, a lot of the time, these difficulties will be so great that the marriage is simply going to fall apart. And since you no longer have any money to do something fun, like go to Las Vegas and gamble, just use your increasingly bitter and declining marital state instead. When the marriage starts to go south, you each write a date on a slip of paper and put it somewhere where you'll remember it. When the financial strain on your marriage becomes completely unbearable, the one who came closest to predicting the actual date wins the remaining foodstuffs in the pantry and the household's supply of loose change.

### Foraging

Just like it sounds: when you get hungry, since you have no money for food, you go out looking for berries and twigs and half-eaten meals in the trash.

This one has an added element of excitement, since some of the things you will eat could kill you.

### What Am I Missing?

All you need for this one is an open-minded doctor with a, let's say, flexible sense of ethics (if you can't find one in your area, check to see if Senator Bill Frist participates in your HMO network; hell, he may even own your HMO—even better). Everyone knows the market for human organs is booming, and it's only likely to get bigger in the future. The top 1 percent may own almost the entire country, but the one thing they don't have yet is immortality. In 1999, a man named Dennis Prince put a listing for a kidney on eBay. Bidding went up to $3 million before the listing was finally pulled.

Even if you don't get that much, it's a pretty sweet deal. And it can be a fun game. Get a doctor to remove and fence one of your organs—but tell him not to tell you which organ it was.

Over the next few weeks, you'll have lots of fun monitoring your symptoms and trying to figure out what you're missing.

Short of breath? Could be a lung you're missing, but can also be your kidney. The possibilities are endless.

### Heavy Drinking

This one requires a little bit of money but can be quite effective. This is how it works: buy a lot of cheap alcohol. Drink it.

# DEBTOR'S PRISON

Even before the passage of Bush's Bankruptcy Enhancement Act, bankruptcy was already one of the hottest trends of the Bush years, going up 10 percent a year during his first term. And 2004 was the best year for the credit card companies in fifteen years, with $30 billion in profit.

But after Bush signed the bill, bankruptcy became practically—in fact, for many, literally—irresistible.

One amendment after another to try to lessen the impact of the bill was voted down, including one to protect military families, one simply to require greater disclosure by the credit card companies about the implications of paying the minimum amount due with high interest rates, one to close the loopholes—widened by the bill—that allowed wealthy people to protect their assets in "protection trusts," one to protect those who are declaring bankruptcy because they're caregivers to ill or disabled family members, one to protect people whose financial difficulty is caused by identity theft, and even one to protect those who had just been hit by a natural disaster.

And if you're a victim of Hurricane Katrina, this means you. After the hurricane hit, several Democratic House members tried to introduce legislation that would exempt the victims of Katrina from the harshest provisions of the bill, which took effect a little over a month after the hurricane. The chair of the House Judiciary Committee, Congressman James Sensenbrenner from Wisconsin, wouldn't even hold a hearing. His reaction? The Katrina criers "ought to get over it."

If you don't know Congressman Sensenbrenner, this probably means you're not a banker, a senior credit card company official, or one of their paid lobbyists. Because these people know him well; they have given him around $90,000 in campaign contributions since 1989. And now their investment in him seems to have borne fruit.

And what, specifically, were the Democratic congressmen objecting to? Things like, say, the part of the bill that requires petitioners to go through a complicated "means test," which involves lots of paperwork, records, bank stubs, utility bills. When your house has floated away, or just been destroyed, those things are hard to come by. Too bad. But at least now you don't have to hunt for them.

And this fall, the French company Euler Hermès, which provides credit insurance to businesses worldwide, predicts that in 2006, business failures in the United States will rise for the first time since 2000.

For some people, the new bill will mean they can't get out of bankruptcy; for many others, it will mean they're broke but can't get *into* bankruptcy.

Put all this together and what does it mean? Two words: debtor's prison.

They're not only back, but a few more "banking reform bills" down the road there's a good chance you're going to be spending some time in one.

Just think of it like a vacation, only a mandatory one. And a good way to escape the housing bubble. If you still have friends who aren't in debtor's prisons, and you feel embarrassed about telling them, just tell them you're going "to rehab." This excuse can be enhanced if, in the months before your "intake day," you do actually develop a drug or alcohol habit. Then your debtor's-prison experience really will be rehab. Sure it will last considerably longer than the usual thirty-day rehab stay, but by the time that comes around, your friends will have forgotten about you anyway, as they'll be spending much of their time and energy trying not to join you.

So is debtor's prison a real prison? In many respects, yes, though there are a few differences. Most of the debtor's prisons will be run by the credit card companies themselves, who will contract with the government. After all, they pretty much own you, so why should some other privatized prison company get to profit from locking you up?

The other major difference between debtor's prisons and regular prisons is that with regular prisons, some people get out.

That's right. The same policies that led you to be incarcerated will continue on the inside. This means you'll never be leaving. The good news is that questions like "how will I adjust to the outside," "will I be able to get a job as an ex-con," "will I really stay in touch with my cellie" needn't bother you.

The other great thing about debtor's prison is that once you're there, yes, of course, you're going to go deeper into debt, as the interest rate on what you owe the company skyrockets, and they garnish the meager wages you get from whatever menial labor you're assigned, but there's nowhere else to go. Since you'll never pay off the debt, you can stop trying.

If looked at the right way, debtor's prison robs you of your personal freedom, but it liberates you from debt. For life.

# 9 · THE REPUBLICAN NEUROLOGICAL DISORDER PROMOTION ACT OF 2005

There are still a few liberals out there, warning that regulatory agencies like the EPA and the FDA, which protect the consumer and keep our food and air and water safe, will be abolished. And, sure, the market fundamentalists believe that these agencies "inhibit" corporate growth. After all, health and safety concerns don't do much for the immediate bottom line.

But their worry is misplaced. Not because the market fundies are having some crisis of conscience, but because they're too smart to get rid of the agencies altogether. That would just get a lot of bad press (even this press might give them trouble on something like that), and use up a lot of political capital. Plus, they've found a way to do about the same amount of harm while getting credit for doing something good.

What they do is maintain the regulatory agencies but cripple them, trusting that the industries in question will regulate themselves.

A perfect example is the story of mercury—the stuff in your old thermometers. It's also the stuff that, when there is enough of it in the air, causes all sorts of birth defects and neurological damage to children. Limiting the amount of mercury that's released into the air as a by-product of the manufacture of some industrial products is the focus of the Republican Neurological Disorder Promotion Act of 2005, the more honest title for a bill that Republicans call the "Clear Sky Initiative."

Truth be told, we don't think that Republicans want to promote neurological disorders, though it would probably help them electorally. But they don't seem to care that a few hundred thousand neurological disorders might result from loosening standards on these industries. Hey, if you want to make an omelet, you have to break a few skulls.

On March 15, 2005, the Bush administration proudly unveiled new regulations that called for coal-fired power plants to cut their mercury emissions by 22 percent by the year 2010. Good for them, right? Well, the truth is more complicated than that, and we better get it out now, while we still have the brain capacity to understand it.

Mercury is a known neurotoxin. It has been linked to increased autism rates in children—one study has shown that for every thousand pounds of mercury emitted into the environment, autism rates increase by 61 percent. In the United States, each year power plants alone pump fifty tons into the air, from where it often settles in the water, and then in fish, which absorb it. That's why in 2004 the FDA warned pregnant women to stay away from eating all big ocean fish—because the mercury the fish had absorbed could seriously endanger a baby's development.

Mercury has been shown to cause deafness, blindness, mental retardation, and cerebral palsy in children. In high doses, mercury exposure can cause numbness, dementia, and death in adults. Some say that even small amounts of mercury exposure can cause attention deficit disorder in children and Parkinson's in adults. The *American Heart Association Journal* suggests that eating fish with high mercury content can also increase heart disease in middle-aged men.

In February 2005, about a month before President Bush announced his new mercury "reforms," the inspector general of the EPA reported that "the agency's senior management instructed staff members to arrive at a predetermined conclusion favoring industry when they prepared a proposed rule last year to reduce the amount of mercury emitted from coal-fired power plants." The technological and scientific analysis by the agency was "compromised" to keep cleanup costs down for the utility industry. The report said the agency's staff was instructed to determine that the best pollution-control methods available to power-plant owners would cut mercury emissions to 34 million tons from 48 million tons, a result that was approximated only on the third time the agency made its computer calculations. The earlier results showed that this technology might achieve greater reductions, but these were rebuffed by senior managers, the report said.

It concluded that the agency should go back to the drawing board and "conduct an unbiased analysis of the mercury emissions data."* And this from a guy who works or, possibly in light of this report, worked, at the agency.

So not only did the EPA fudge the numbers to make it look harder than it actually is to control emissions, a month later, the Government Accountability Office issued a report saying that the EPA studies that promoted the Bush "market-based" Clear Skies Initiative scheme "distorted the analysis of its controversial proposal to regulate mercury pollution from power plants, making it appear that the Bush administration's market-based approach was superior to a competing scheme supported by environmentalists."†

That's how a "reform" of 22 percent can actually be not such a good thing, which some media outlets noted at the time:

> The Bush administration Tuesday told the operators of coal-fired power plants to cut mercury emissions by nearly 22 percent over the next five years, hailing the reductions as the deepest cuts technologically possible for cleansing the air of the neurological toxin.
>
> But nearly a dozen power plants nationwide have done far better

---

* "E.P.A. Accused of a Predetermined Finding on Mercury," Felicity Barringer, *New York Times,* February 4, 2005, Section A, page 16.

† "EPA Distorted Mercury Analysis, GAO Says," Shankar Vedantam, *Washington Post,* March 8, 2005, page A09.

already—some cutting mercury emissions by as much as 94 percent—in test projects paid for by the same Bush administration.*

---

## PROPOSAL: REFORM REFORM

The Republicans love reform. Or, rather, "reform." They figured out that if you call something "reform," or attach other feel-good language to something bad, it seems good. And a lot of the media will adopt the language you do, and continue the good feeling. There's the "Clear Skies Initiative" that makes the skies less clear, the "Healthy Forests Initiative" that makes the forests less healthy, "Tax Relief" that increases the burden on everyone not in the top income percentiles, "Social Security Reform" that, in Bush's version, was a way to reform Social Security right out of existence. The list goes on and on. So here's our proposal: we need a reform reform. It's clear that reform has become badly broken. It simply isn't working. And if we don't fix reform now, what are our children and our grandchildren going to use when something is broken and needs to be fixed or improved? We need you to write your representatives and urge them to pass the comprehensive Reform Reform Bill.

---

So you have EPA-sponsored and paid-for tests that show mercury-emission reductions could easily be twice as large as Bush's much-trumpeted rules—and then you have Bush's EPA spokesperson say, "Over the next five or six years, these are the fastest reductions" possible.

Someone should have told Wisconsin, which joined a lawsuit with ten other states because the federal rules actually *required* the states to allow more mercury into the air than their current legislation allows for. That

---

* "New Mercury Rules Announced; Levels Lag Behind Current Reduction," Seth Borenstein, Knight Ridder Newspapers, March 15, 2005.

bears repeating: the federal regulations "reform" that Bush trumpets actually requires some states to allow more poison into our air. In fact, in Wisconsin's case, that means they have to allow nearly twice as much mercury to be emitted in the next ten years as they would have under their current laws. Viva clear skies! And not so viva people!

## OTHER FUN THINGS TO DO
## WITH NEUROLOGICAL DAMAGE

★ Watch Fox News and *believe.*

★ Dress like Congresswoman Jean Schmidt.

★ Write new verses to a Toby Keith song. Like this:

*Hey, America,*
*Top of the world, you're A-number-one*
*And, hey, Washington Monument*
*If I look sideways, you look like a gun.*
*The eagle will soar*
*And strike tremendous fear*
*In all humans anyplace but here*
*The Red White and Blue falling from the sky*
*With a burst of freedom landing on you*
*Always makes me cry.*
*Yeah.*

★ Masturbate in public.

★ Unofficially "patrol" the Mexican border.

★ Eat shoes.

★ Call someone and invite them to take a shower with you in the Caribbean.

★ Hang out socially with Robert Novak.

★ Constantly assume you're in a pool swimming.

# JUST BECAUSE YOU CAN'T THINK DOESN'T MEAN YOU CAN'T HAVE FUN

It looks like for the foreseeable future, there's gonna be a lot of mercury in the air. And that means there's gonna be a lot of neurological damage. But maybe because we're just cockeyed optimists, or maybe because we're actually brain-damaged ourselves, we believe that severe neurological damage is all in how you look at it.

Here's the glass-full-of-mercury way of seeing things . . .

## FUN THINGS ABOUT NEUROLOGICAL DAMAGE

### We're All in This Together

Since we're all going to be neurologically impaired, you won't have to worry about the social stigma. Can't remember your best friend's name? That's okay. They don't know who the hell you are, either. So forget about trying to remember each other's name, and put your remaining brain power into something more productive, like trying to figure out where you live or why you're not wearing any pants.

### Staying in Is Fun

If you do find you don't want to go out, or are afraid you'll never find your house again if you do, stay in! Because you know what? Television is suddenly going to seem a lot better. According to our predictions, for every ton of mercury released into the air, the ratings for *According to Jim* will go up 22 percent. Don't have HBO? You won't even miss it. The problem here is going to be not what to watch, but what not to watch. The Weather Channel, *Punk'd! My Wife and Kids*, a test pattern, even *The Apprentice*: they're all going to seem fantastic. Even better: you won't remember having seen them. Every episode will be new to you—like reruns had never been invented.

### Hey, Look at That!

This is a fun game where you just stare off into space. Can be played for hours, even days, at a time. Remember to eat!

# 10 · LIFE BEGINS . . . JUST BEFORE SEX

Rapture Rightism is a whole-body philosophy—a kind of wellness-care program, only
without so much of the wellness. They're not
concerned just about things like television, curricula, science, facts—
they're also concerned about your body. Especially your genitals. Or, as
they like to say, "down there," or "Satan's Lego Blocks."

And just because they approve of the gender you're having sex with,
doesn't mean they don't want to control how you're doing it. And, no, we're
not talking about positions, though if it comes to that, it's hard to believe
that the "missionary position" doesn't start out with a big advantage with
the Rapture Right.

We're talking about pregnancy. Your pregnancy. Aside from the question of whether or not you'll always be able to end a pregnancy, pretty soon
you may not even be able to prevent a pregnancy.

In fact, the legal rights to both end a pregnancy and not start one have
always been related. The right to privacy *Roe v. Wade* is based on was first
articulated in the 1965 case *Griswold v. Connecticut,* in which the Supreme

Court found that a Connecticut state law prohibiting use of contraception by married adults unconstitutionally inhibited the right to privacy.

Sure, Chief Justice Roberts has said he agrees "with the *Griswold* court's conclusion that marital privacy extends to contraception and availability of that,"* and Justice Samuel Alito, according to Senator Arlen Specter's account of a private meeting with him, described *Griswold* as "good law,"† but that doesn't mean much. Or at least it won't if they're successful doing to contraception what they're doing to abortion.

Yes, they'd love to overturn *Roe*—and they might well still do it, especially with this court—but in the meantime, what they've done is try to make getting an abortion as difficult as possible to get. One-third of all American women now live in counties with no access to abortion, and the number is growing. And likewise with contraception—they want to get rid of it, but they're not going to be so clumsy as to try to overrule *Griswold*. That would attract a lot of publicity. Still, what they can do is, as with abortion, make it as difficult as possible to obtain.

☆ ☆ ☆

## PHARMACISTS OF CONSCIENCE

The old way: you need contraception, you go to your doctor, he writes you a prescription, you take it to the pharmacist, he fills it. The new way: the pharmacist looks at your prescription, decides that you're immoral, and not only refuses to fill the prescription but holds it hostage.

Just a paranoid fantasy? "The trend has opened a new front in the nation's battle over reproductive rights," wrote Rob Stein in the *Washington Post*,‡

---

* Said in testimony, in answer to a question by Wisconsin senator Herb Kohl, as reported in "Campaign for the Supreme Court," Miranda Spivack, *Washington Post*, September 13, 2005.
† "Bush Nominates Samuel Alito for Supreme Court," William Douglas and James Kuhnhenn, Knight Ridder Newspapers, October 31, 2005.
‡ "Pharmacists' Rights at Front of New Debate," Rob Stein, *Washington Post*, March 28, 2005, page A01.

"sparking an intense debate over the competing rights of pharmacists to refuse to participate in something they consider repugnant and a woman's right to get medications her doctor has prescribed." Take, for example, those affiliated with a group called "Pharmacists for Life International"— the Web site of which compares Illinois governor Rod Blagojevich to Slobodan Milošević for directing his state's pharmacists to do their jobs. In this new world, pharmacists claim a right "not only to decline to fill prescriptions themselves but also to refuse to refer customers elsewhere or transfer prescriptions."*

That's what happened to twenty-one-year-old Suzanne Richards. Her prescription for the "morning after" pill was rejected in her hometown pharmacy in Laconia, New Hampshire, late on a Saturday night. By the time she was able to find another drugstore to fill the prescription, the seventy-two-hour efficacy period had expired.† Oh well, there's always prayer.

Similar cases have cropped up in California, Ohio, Illinois, and Texas, where Joe Pojman, executive director of the Texas Alliance for Life, defended denying emergency contraception to rape victims by speculating that the woman probably wouldn't be pregnant anyway: "A woman has gone through a trauma; for these reasons her body may not be fertile."‡

Thanks, doc.

On to Madison, Wisconsin. Neil Noeson was the pharmacist at a K-mart when a woman came in one weekend to refill her birth control pill prescription. Mr. Noeson was curious why the woman was taking the pills (contraceptive pills are used for a wide range of medical issues). When the woman replied that she was taking them so she could have sex without getting pregnant, Mr. Noeson declared that she should get her pills elsewhere.§

At least he asked first, though, right? One hopes that Neil et al. don't start seeing things like sinusitis and the flu as simply "God's will."

---

* Ibid.
† Ibid.
‡ "A Matter of Choice," Parth Gejji, *Daily Texan,* March 2, 2005.
§ "Pharmacist Refused to Fill Birth Control," Associated Press, October 12, 2004.

## SAMPLE PRESCRIPTIONS FROM THE YEAR 2035

**For avian flu:**

4 Hail Marys

2 Hail Dobsons (morning and evening, three times on Sunday)

$2,000 check payable to the American Family Association.

**For birth control pills:**

When aroused, read the following Bible verse out loud:

"Flee fornication. Every sin that a man doeth is without the body; but he that committeth fornication sinneth against his own body."

Continue reading until the urge to sinneth has passed.

**For cancer:**

As cancer is God's will, ask Almighty God to have mercy on your wicked, rotten soul (not to be taken with milk).

So what's a woman to do when denied access to something she assumed she had a legal right to? Go to the police, of course. Which is what she did, and came back to the pharmacy with two police officers in tow. But Neil simply refused to fill her prescription, and the cops did nothing.

Gloria Feldt of Planned Parenthood told *USA Today* in November 2004, "We have always understood that the battles about abortion were just the tip of a larger ideological iceberg, and that it's really birth control that they're after also."*

How big of a jump is it from there to, say, emergency-care workers refusing to give care to gay people?

Not very far.

Though it's not yet illegal to be gay in Michigan, make sure you don't get into a car accident. The Conscientious Objector Policy Act,† passed by the Republican-controlled Michigan House in 2004, states:

> A health care provider may object as a matter of conscience to providing or participating in a health care service on ethical, moral, or religious grounds.

In other words, gay person/unmarried cohabitor/smoker/liberal/Democrat, heal thyself.

\* \* \*

## A MISCARRIAGE OF SOMETHING

So let's say you do become pregnant. But, unfortunately, you miscarry. This happens a lot, especially in the early stages of pregnancy, but that doesn't mean it's not often a wrenching experience. Some people suggest counseling. Others think that you should talk it out with your significant other. Virginia state delegate John Cosgrove thinks that the best thing for you in this difficult time is to go down to the local police station and tell them about it. Think of it as a uniformed—and armed—shoulder to cry on. Or a new sixth step of the grieving process. Here's the text of a bill Cosgrove offered to the Virginia legislature in December 2004:

---

* "Druggists Refuse to Give Out Pill," Charisse Jones, *USA Today*, November 8, 2004, page 3A.
† House Bill 5006, as passed, April 21, 2004.

HB 1677. Report of fetal death by mother; penalty.

Provides that when a fetal death occurs without medical attendance, it shall be the woman's responsibility to report the death to the proper law-enforcement agency within 12 hours of the delivery. Violation of this section shall be punishable as a Class 1 misdemeanor.

But it turns out Cosgrove had jumped the gun a bit. He was hit by a firestorm of criticism—largely from liberal bloggers—which forced him to clarify the language of his bill so that it would apply only to full-term births that went unattended by medical professionals. He also added that "the tone of the e-mails has been disgusting." He later withdrew the bill altogether. Well, there's always tomorrow.

It really doesn't matter at what stage they get you. Your "product of conception" is not your own—regardless of what form it's in. It's only a matter of time before they want to control the elements of conception themselves (guys, it might be time to think twice before you get into the shower with thoughts of that new Victoria's Secret catalog in your filthy head).

In fact, maybe you just shouldn't have sex at all . . .

# 11 · ABSTINENCE ONLY:
# The Oral and Anal Sex Enhancement Initiative

George Bush made some real hay in Texas with his "abstinence only" programs. The advantage to them is that they significantly cut down on the need for complicated and costly studies of human biology and sexual responsibility in high school curricula. The stated goal of abstinence-only programs is to prevent risky sexual behavior by teens. And the great thing is, they work perfectly. Until they don't. Which is often.

But that hasn't stopped Bush from increasing funding for abstinence-only programs by nearly $200 million, even as he's cut real education funding, including Pell Grants, and underfunded his own "No Child Left Behind" project.

In 2005, researchers at Texas A&M University delivered a study* on abstinence-only programs to the Texas Department of State Health Services. "We didn't see any strong indications that these programs were having an

---

* Reuters, "Texas Teens Increased Sex After Abstinence Program," February 1, 2005.

impact in the direction desired," said Dr. Buzz Pruitt, who directed the study. The doc was understating the results.

Before enrolling in the abstinence program, 23 percent of ninth-grade girls had sex. After going through the program, 29 percent of the same girls reported that they'd had sex. With the boys, the increase went from 24 to 39 percent.

It gets worse.

Early in 2005, an eight-year-long study by the National Longitudinal Study of Adolescent Health tracked twenty thousand young people from high school to early adulthood to see how abstinence-only and "virginity pledges" affected the behavior of the "adherents."* The results? Let us put it this way: if you're a horny seventeen-year-old, you should be out right now looking for someone who has signed a "virginity pledge."

The study found that teens taking the pledge were more than five times more likely to have oral or anal sex. Makes sense. They're just adhering to the letter of the law. Teens sworn to abstinence more frequently maintain their "technical virginity" by abstaining from vaginal sex and instead seek out alternatives.

The virginity pledges did not make a significant difference in the prevention of STDs—adolescents who pledged abstinence were almost as likely to contract STDs as kids who didn't.

But all that scientific mumbo jumbo doesn't bother Bill Pierce, spokesman of the Department of Health and Human Services. As he told the AP, "One thing we do know about abstinence is that if you practice it, you will not have an unintended pregnancy or risk catching a sexually transmitted disease."†

Clearly Mr. Pierce is not acquainted with how the idea of sex—any kind of sex—can, let's say, focus the reasoning powers of your average teenage boy.

And even to the extent that you can get the teens to maintain some sort

---

* "Virginity Pledges Aren't as Effective as Sex Education," Celeste DeFreitas, *Daily Trojan*, April 6, 2005.

† "Government Abstinence Site Draws Fire," Associated Press, April 1, 2005.

of technical virginity, there's the question of how you do it. It turns out, the kids would be better off abstaining from the class:

> Many American youngsters participating in federally funded abstinence-only programs have been taught over the past three years that abortion can lead to sterility and suicide, that half the gay male teenagers in the United States have tested positive for the AIDS virus, and that touching a person's genitals "can result in pregnancy," a congressional staff analysis has found.*

The study was commissioned by Congressman Henry Waxman of California. Here are a few other things Waxman's investigators discovered:

* ★ A forty-three-day-old fetus is a "thinking person"

* ★ HIV, the virus that causes AIDS, can be spread via sweat and tears

* ★ Condoms fail to prevent HIV transmission as often as 31 percent of the time in heterosexual intercourse†

Of course, how effective can you be teaching about sexuality when you can't even bring yourself to say the word "condom"? Here's Leslie Unruh, the founder of a group called Abstinence Clearinghouse:

> We really want to plead to the Bush administration and to all of those who are taking the federal funding . . . let's clean this up and let's get rid of the contraception and let's get rid of the "C" message . . .‡

The good news is you still can't get pregnant from sitting in a hot tub. But if you're a guy, and you're sporting a big "E" message because of a woman's "V" message, be sure and wear a "C" message.

---

\* "Some Abstinence Programs Mislead Teens, Report Says," Ceci Connolly, *Washington Post*, December 2, 2004, page A01.
† Ibid.
‡ Bill Francher, Agape Press, January 6, 2006, via the blog Pam's House Blend, at pamspaulding.com.

# I WANT MY HPV

Here's something you won't hear much about in sex ed: HPV. That's short for the human papilloma virus, a sexually transmitted disease that, when left untreated, is one of the most significant factors in the development of cervical cancer. HPV is extremely common; half of all sexually active women between ages eighteen and twenty-two in the United States have it.* The incidence of cervical cancer is expected to jump four times by 2050. But HPV is also very preventable. In fact, a vaccine against the disease is about to be approved. That is, unless the Bush administration has its way.

Why would anyone have a problem with vaccinating women against an STD that could lead to cancer?

"Abstinence is the best way to prevent HPV," says Bridget Maher of the Family Research Council, a leading Christian lobby group. "Giving the HPV vaccine to young women could be potentially harmful, because they may see it as a license to engage in premarital sex," Maher claims.

One can just imagine the chaos erupting in the halls of high schools all over the country. "I was immunized against the human papilloma virus—let's get it on!"

---

* "Will Cancer Vaccine Get to All Women?" Debora MacKenzie, April 18, 2005, NewScientist.com news service.

# 12 · THE SECRETARY OF LOVE

The following is an online question-and-answer column by the United States secretary of human intimacy, Rick Santorum. The weekly forum is open to the public at www.whitehouse.humanintimacy.gov/Secretaryoflove.html.

Note from Secretary Santorum: In regards to human intimacy, I am what is known as an "originalist." That is, I am someone who doesn't believe in legislating from the cabinet seat. I make my decisions and policies according to what I see as the original intent of The Framer of Human Intimacy, the Original Founding Father: Yahweh.

Why is the discussion being held online? Because, as our Constitution says—in Ephesians 5:12—"It is shameful even to mention the things these people do in secret." Notice that the text says "mention." It says nothing about online discussion, and, since, as I stated, I am an originalist, typing is therefore okay. I am here because I feel it is one of the duties of my office to help guide people to a more full expression of human intimacy, as the Founder of Our Country intended.

## SUSAN, LINCOLN, NEBRASKA:

**Dear Secretary Santorum:** My husband refuses to make love to me when I am having my period. How can I convince him that it's not "gross" or "weird"?

**SECRETARY SANTORUM:** Susan, your husband is wrong. It is neither gross nor weird.

**SUSAN:** So he should just get over it, you mean?

**SECRETARY SANTORUM:** No, he's right about not having sex with you during your period. Not because it's gross, but more because it's unclean. As the giver of our laws, the ultimate "Chief Justice" states: "If a woman have an issue, and her issue in her flesh be blood, she shall be put apart seven days: and whosoever toucheth her shall be unclean until the even." (Leviticus 15:19)

So, not only should he not lie with you while you're having your issue, you must leave the city. And not just the technical city limits, but the entire city, out past the airport. To ensure you comply, you may take one of the Menses Minibuses that we have installed in every major city. The fare is free—all you need to board is proof of your issue, and then it's all aboard!

Once on the menarche motorcoach, you will be taken to one of the Unclean Encampments, where you will stay until finished with your issue. The camps themselves are really more like spas, however. In fact, if you're anything like Mrs. Santorum, you probably won't even want to go back. Your day will be filled with such activities as singing, sewing, and praying to Almighty God that He forgive the filthy uncleanliness that you bring into the world each month.

Hope that helps.

## *BILLY, RALEIGH, NORTH CAROLINA:*

**Dear Secretary Santorum:** Does sex hurt?

**SECRETARY SANTORUM:** Only if you're doing it right.

**BILLY:** Really? You mean it's supposed to hurt?

**SECRETARY SANTORUM:** Only the woman. It's called God's Will: "Unto the woman he said, I will greatly multiply thy sorrow and thy conception; in sorrow thou shalt bring forth children; and thy desire shall be to thy husband, and he shall rule over thee." (Genesis 3:16)

## *JUDITH, RIVERSIDE, CALIFORNIA:*

**Dear Secretary Santorum:** My husband recently cheated on me. We've been working through it, but when it comes to sex, I just can't enjoy it. Can you help?

**SECRETARY SANTORUM:** Actually, Judith, your problem is very easily solved.

**JUDITH:** How? What should I do?

**SECRETARY SANTORUM:** Your husband must be stoned.

**JUDITH:** I don't think marijuana is going to help. We're not into that sort of thing.

**SECRETARY SANTORUM:** No, I mean, he must be stoned. With rocks. To death.

**JUDITH:** That seems a bit extreme. Surely something else can be done.

**SECRETARY SANTORUM:** You're right. If the other woman was married, she must be put to death also. It's right there in the law: "If a man is found sleeping with another man's wife, both the man who slept with her and the woman must die." (Deuteronomy 22:22)

*DAN, SEATTLE, WASHINGTON:*

**Dear Secretary Santorum:** The other day, my wife caught me looking at a pornographic magazine and got upset. Now she's saying I have to throw it out, but I think it's normal. Who's right?

**SECRETARY SANTORUM:** Fortunately, Dan, we can look to established precedent here. As the official at whose pleasure I serve—Almighty God—said, ". . . whosoever looketh on a woman to lust after her hath committed adultery with her already in his heart.

"And if thy right eye offend thee, pluck it out, and cast it from thee: for it is profitable for thee that one of thy members should perish, and not that thy whole body should be cast into hell."

**DAN:** So you're saying I shouldn't look at it?

**SECRETARY SANTORUM:** No. I mean, yes. I mean you should first pluck your eye out, so you won't be able to look at it anyway.

And don't forget to cast it from thee after you pluck it out.

Are you still there, Dan?

**DAN:** Yes.

**SECRETARY SANTORUM:** That's not all you have to do. The law in question states quite clearly that once you looked at the pornography, you have already committed adultery, so you must also be stoned. Our human-intimacy officers have your location from your IP address and they'll be around shortly. Perhaps you'll meet

Judith's husband. On the plus side, this will save your whole body from being cast into hell. Thanks for your question.

## EVIE, LITTLE ROCK, ARKANSAS:

**Dear Secretary Santorum:** I'm fourteen years old, and my boyfriend and I were fooling around recently. We didn't go all the way, but I'm late for my period. Is it possible to get pregnant without having sex?

**SECRETARY SANTORUM:** Ever hear of a woman named Mary?

**EVIE:** You mean Mary in my third period homeroom? I did hear she was pretty slutty.

**SECRETARY SANTORUM:** No, I mean Mary the Mother of Jesus, our president emeritus. She got pregnant without having sex. And also, I might add, without fooling around.

**EVIE:** Oh my God, so you mean I might be pregnant then?

**SECRETARY SANTORUM:** Unlikely, but that's up to the Lord.

**EVIE:** So what should I do?

**SECRETARY SANTORUM:** Get married as soon as possible and pray for forgiveness that our attorney general, the Holy Spirit, doesn't hurl your souls into eternal hellfire. Oh, and mazel tov!

## LINDA, SPRINGFIELD, MASSACHUSETTS:

**Dear Secretary Santorum:** My husband and I don't have sex much anymore. When we were first married, it was all the time, and really intense. Now we both get home from work, put the kids to bed, and just want to go to sleep. How can we "rekindle the magic" we once had?

**SECRETARY SANTORUM:** Well, Linda, the first is easy: stop working.

**LINDA:** But we need the extra income. And I like my job.

**SECRETARY SANTORUM:** Yeah, sin is very fun. That's why people do it. You can either take care of your family and lead a spiritually and sexually healthy life, or carpool with Satan on the way to work. It's your choice. At least until we pass HR 2418, which we've just sent up to the Hill.

Well, that's all the time we have. Barring the Rapture, I'll see you next week.

# 13 · I HATE MYSELF:
## Life as a Gay Republican

Whether the Rapture Republicans "hate" gays is debatable. We're just kidding—of course it isn't. Reading too much of the mainstream media will sometimes make you say that sort of thing.

There was much talk about how in the 2004 election Karl Rove was able to cynically use homophobia as a wedge issue, flogging it in churches across the country as a way to increase turnout among evangelical voters.

But this is unfair. This is no "election tactic." This is heartfelt stuff—to an almost pathological degree. Homosexuality—the very idea of it, fear of it, control of it—is deeply embedded in the DNA of the Rapture Right. It's like a National Geographic channel documentary about a remote tribe whose entire society—food, fuel, currency, religion, rituals—is based solely on a single animal. Like the Eskimos and whales—that's what homosexuality is to the Rapture Right. It defines them, it nurtures them, it gets them through the winter. Even though they profess to hate it, you wonder what they'd do without it.

But here's the catch: they hate gay people only to the extent that they believe there *are* gay people. In Rapture Right world, there are only: (1) good people—those who *choose* not to do gay things, and (2) bad people— those who *choose* to do gay things.

What this means, it follows, is that we all have gay inclinations, and only some of us are able to resist. But just because someone really believes this, doesn't that kind of make *them* gay?

Yes. It does.

It's like this: they see the urge to be gay and do gay things as having a sweet tooth. Almost everyone has a bit of a sweet tooth, they say, only some people have a stronger sweet tooth than others. You either choose to indulge it or you don't. What it comes down to is that the Rapture Right sees the gay lifestyle as being really, really sweet. Rich, chocolaty sweet.

Just listen to Dr. Paul Cameron, founder of the Family Research Institute and ISIS, the Institute for the Scientific Investigation of Sexuality, a guy with a really, really big sweet tooth. He's kind of the guru of antigayism. All the Rapture Rightists love this guy—in a very straight way, of course, because he's a doctor, and also because he's completely off his not-at-all-gay rocker.

> If you isolate sexuality as something solely for one's own personal amusement, and all you want is the most satisfying orgasm you can get—and that is what homosexuality seems to be—then *homosexuality seems too powerful to resist.* The evidence is that men do a better job on men and women on women, if all you are looking for is orgasm . . . I'm convinced that lesbians are particularly good seducers . . . It's pure sexuality. *It's almost like pure heroin. It's such a rush.* They are committed in almost a religious way. And they'll take enormous risks, do anything . . . *Marital sex tends toward the boring end, . . . generally, it doesn't deliver the kind of sheer sexual pleasure that homosexual sex does.*[*]

---

[*] "The Holy War on Gays," Robert Dreyfuss, *Rolling Stone*, March 18, 1999.

The emphasis is ours—mostly to suggest that if there is a Mrs. Cameron, she may want to look into seeing whether that prenup is airtight. Sounds a bit like the good doctor, like all good doctors, has simply been doing a lot of clinical research.

But to the Rapture Right, gay sex acts aren't just normal chocolate cake—they're evil chocolate cake, dirty, dirty, evil chocolate cake, with evil-flavored frosting and luscious evil cream-filling with naughty evil-tasting raspberry sauce dripping down its sides. Not easy to resist.

This might be a good time for the reader to go have a snack. Or masturbate.

Welcome back. We hope you feel better, but not, you know, too sleepy to continue reading.

Now, given that being gay—or, rather, we should say, *acting* gay (as in having gay sex)—is ~~the best thing ever like pure heroin oh my god I can't believe it I've never felt more alive~~ very bad in our new country, and that we can expect the attacks on it to get even worse, what if you feel like you're not just gay-acting, but you really are gay? What should you do? Relax. There are plenty of good options.

First: stop being gay.

Yes, we realize that might seem difficult. Fortunately, there's help for you. Just think of it like this: you're gay because you happened to get mixed up with the wrong people (gay people). The gay people made you be gay. All you need to do is spend your time with different people—join a new club. And the good news is that these already exist—groups whose sole purpose is to put you on the straight and very narrow.

\* \* \*

## EXODUS: FLEEING FROM YOURSELF AS GOD HAS COMMANDED

Exodus is one of the largest of the many organizations that will helpfully convert you from a gay person into a normal person. According to its Web site, Exodus is a nonprofit, interdenominational Christian organization promoting the message of "Freedom from homosexuality through the power of Jesus Christ."

But wait, does this mean that Muslims, Jews, Buddhists, Hindus, and agnostics who are "affected by homosexuality" must accept Jesus Christ or keep living in sin?

Yes.

And if you don't happen to live near an Exodus group, don't worry, there are plenty of gay conversion groups out there. In fact, many economists predict that gay conversion is set to become the next "hot" growth industry. New ones are popping up all over the country. Here's a list of some. Some names are real, some are still out there for the taking. Can you guess which are which? (Answers below.)*

* Love in Action

* Erection Redirection

* Homosexuals Anonymous

* Courage!

* Desert Stream

* I Hate Myself

* NARTH: National Association of Research and Therapy of Homosexuality

* Gaybegone

* One by One

* PFOX: Parents and Friends of Ex-Gays

* People Can Change

---

* Real: Love in Action, Courage, Desert Stream, NARTH, One by One, PFOX, People Can Change.

★ The Closet Window

★ ButtOut

★ No More Backsliding

Though ex-gay conferences and families-of-ex-gay conferences remain very profitable—helped by the tremendous amount of scorn and shame heaped on gay teens (you gotta create a market)—becoming an ex-gay, it turns out, isn't always the end of the story.

If you happen to be acquainted with any non-guilt-ridden gay people, you won't be surprised to learn that there tend to be a lot of ex-gays in the ex-gay community who subsequently become ex-ex-gays.

Take the story of John Paulk. He wasn't just any ex-gay. He was chairman of the board of Exodus International, and on the staff of Focus on the Family. Back in 1998, John was the ex-gay subject of a *Newsweek* cover, along with his ex-lesbian wife.

You may notice that this was an even year, which means it was an election year, which is a special time when the Rapture Right turns up the heat on gays to whip up its supporters. (There's been some speculation that this strategy has run its course, that there is no more election juice to be wrung out of the right wing with the gay baiting. That speculation has turned out to be wrong.)*

And who better to front this strategy than an ex-gay? Gives a little cover, a little gay street cred. So John wrote a book titled *Not Afraid to Change: The Remarkable Story of How One Man Overcame Homosexuality*. The book became a success. John's becoming a former homosexual was somewhat less of a success.

Less than two years later, a few staffers for the gay rights group Human Rights Campaign literally bumped into him in a famous gay bar in

---

* In 2004, the GOP placed antigay marriage referendums on eleven state ballots and, of course, you may remember George Bush's press conference announcing support for an amendment to the Constitution banning gay marriage.

Washington, D.C., called Mr. P's. After Mr. Paulk offered to buy one of them a drink, they took some photos of him in the bar.

Turns out, cruising gay bars without the "intent to heal" is a big no-no in the ex-gay community. And so, John was cast out of Exodus, or at least his position on the North American Board. They were apparently not satisfied with John's explanation that he had simply wandered into the bar because he had to use the bathroom and that "once I was inside, I thought 'Oh, this is a gay bar, I probably shouldn't be in here.'" A simple urinary-locational homosexual mishap. He stayed for only forty short minutes. And he left once he realized his mistake. But he should be more careful in the future; you know how chocolate cake is—one bite and the next thing you know you're in the back alley with your pants around your ankles taking the Lord's name in vain.

Paulk is, of course, not the only ex-gay in the ex-gay community to find it more satisfying to live as an ex-ex-gay.* Exodus was founded at a 1976 California conference of ex-gay ministries organized by two ex-gay counselors, Gary Cooper and Michael Bussee. As it turns out, Exodus wasn't the only thing to blossom at the conference. Later, on tour with Exodus, Bussee and Cooper admitted they were no longer ex-gay but ex-ex-gay, and madly in love with each other. They both divorced their wives and beat a hasty exodus from Exodus.†

Aside from the incredibly high incidence of "recidivism," and the requirement that you mention Jesus' name hundreds of times a day, there isn't necessarily anything wrong with Exodus or groups like them. They provide a way to deal with the painful situation for Rapture Christians who happen to be gay, or at least incapable of resisting doing gay things. Instead of living their lives in shame, secretly denying who they are, they now have the opportunity to deny who they are publicly.

And for those many ex-gays who will shortly become ex-ex-gays, and

---

* Though he may, in fact, be an ex-ex-ex-gay now—it's hard to keep up.

† FYI: Sam has already pitched this scenario as a sitcom. No luck so far, but fingers crossed.

even more for those gays who are just happy being gay, as evidence has shown, gay conversions turn out to be great pickup joints.

* * *

## ALL HOPE IS NOT LOST

In the event that you can't contain these urges, you can't somehow "fix" yourself, you're scared about getting a lobotomy, or your HMO won't cover electroshock therapy, all hope is not lost.

What if we were to tell you that you can have all the gay sex you want and not even be gay? You read correctly: you can have all sorts of gay sexual experiences and not only not be gay, but actually be antigay. How? you ask. Easy. With virtually no repression, just a smidgen of deep-seated self-loathing and the help of some very prominent past and present Republicans, we can show you how to enjoy the gay lifestyle while being totally and 100 percent antigay.

But first, let's lay our cards on the table, shall we?

### The Gay Realization

You look in the mirror. You say, "Hey, I'm a Republican. I have a job. I am married. I like football. I find *Queer Eye* too gay. When my wife complains a lot, or starts acting suspicious, or starts sublimating her sex drive into picking annoying fights, I break down and have sex with her. But generally she's happy as long as I buy her things and don't mention her massive drinking problem.

"Put that all together. I am not homosexual. That thing that happened in the men's bathroom in the park that night was a total misunderstanding. I am not homosexual. And that time I went to that place out on old Route 43 with the red velvet door and no sign and met that guy and we went into the cornfield? That was really about our mutual not-at-all-gay interest in monster truck competitions. I am not homosexual.

So what if I really enjoy *Sex and the City*. I am not—oh my God, please

# ALL HOMOPHOBES GAY, STUDY FINDS

Now that you're starting to feel like you've got your life all sorted out as an antigay gay, the question may occasionally occur to you: wait, I hate gays, and yet I am gay. Isn't that weird? That's a natural question, a sign of a healthy, inquisitive, rabidly anti-gay mind. Even better news, the answer is no, it's not strange. In fact, you practically have no choice. Don't blame yourself, blame science.

You know how when you watch the news and there's some right-wing guy going off on gay people, and then, years later, it turns out that that person is really gay, and you think, "Wow, are all gay-haters gay? I wonder if anybody has ever done a real scientific study on it. I would sure like to see something like that!" Well, you're never going to believe this, but . . .

In 1996, three scientists from the University of Georgia— Henry E. Adams, Ph.D., Lester W. Wright Jr., Ph.D., and Bethany A. Lohr—published a study called "Is Homophobia Associated With Homosexual Arousal?" in the *Journal of Abnormal Psychology*, published by the American Psychological Association.

The study involved twenty-nine nonhomophobic men, and thirty-five homophobic men, as determined by something called the Index of Homophobia scale. All sixty-four men described themselves as completely straight.

Each man was shown three kinds of videotapes (for free): heterosexual, male homosexual, and lesbian. While they watched, they were hooked up to something called a penile plethysmograph, which measures male tumescence, a fancy word for an erection.*

There was no difference between the two groups of men while they were watching the heterosexual videos or the lesbian videos. But here's where it gets interesting. While watching the male homosexual videos, the homophobic men were more than twice as likely to be aroused as the nonhomophobic men—54 to 24 percent. Only 20 percent of the homophobic men showed little or no arousal while watching the homosexual videos.

What's more, when asked to give their own verbal opinion about their arousal, the nonhomophobic men were fairly accurate for all these kinds of videos. The homophobic men were accurate for only two of the video categories. They significantly underestimated their arousal for the other category. Can you guess which one that was?

So what does all this mean? For one thing, it means it's perfectly natural to be really, really antigay and yet be gay. But does it mean that all homophobes are actually gay? Yes. It does.

_____

* If you are, in fact, secretly gay, stay away from these machines—they're nothing but trouble for you.

Lord help me! I've already attended all the God Squad ex-gay institutes and I'm still an ex-ex-gay. Please Sam and Stephen, HELP ME!"

Congratulations! You realize you're gay. Just don't tell anyone! Hang on to that lump of self-loathing—cherish it, nurture it. It will keep you ashamed enough to be quiet and not blow your cover (unless, of course, your cover is that cute Hispanic boy who works at the produce counter of your local Quick Mart). To keep all this bursting confusion under wraps you're going to have to transfer the struggle—and all that loathing—from yourself onto the world around you.

### Spread the Hate

You're angry. You don't want to be gay. Why should you? When you were growing up, your daddy and mommy taught you gays were evil. The bully at school used to pick on you and call you "faggot." (By the way, he's gay, too.) Or maybe you were the bully. In any case, you're feeling a lot of self-loathing right now. In fact, you've probably been feeling it for a while. It explains the drinking issues and why you killed the neighbor's dog that one time.

You must learn to refocus that self-loathing outward—toward the people who are managing their "crisis" better than you, toward people who don't even think they have a crisis in the first place. Those people are the true crazy ones. Not you.

★ ★ ★

## PROFILES IN SELF-HATING GAY COURAGE

Gay-tolerators like to talk a lot about "role models," prominent gays or gay-tolerators whose bravery and dedication have paved the way for other gays and gay-tolerators by making them realize it is possible to be openly gay or gay-tolerating and lead a successful life. But what about me, you say, a gay person who hates gays? Where are my role models? Is it possible to climb to the top of antigay circles while still being gay? Rest easy. You have role models, too. Here are just some of the courageous gay men who, when society said "Wait, antigay person, aren't you gay? Shouldn't you stop being antigay?" proudly replied: "No."*

## Roy Cohn

The granddaddy of them all. He had it all: he was deeply gay, deeply antigay. You can't talk about self-hating homosexuals without talking about Roy Cohn. He might well be the Rosa Parks of the gay antigay movement.

As a young prosecutor in the Manhattan U.S. Attorney's office, he specialized in going after suspected Communists. He was most proud of the role he played in the conviction, and subsequent execution, of Julius and Ethel Rosenberg.

He soon caught the eye of FBI head J. Edgar Hoover (insert your own joke here), who recommended Cohn—over another candidate, Robert F. Kennedy—to be the chief counsel for the Investigations Subcommittee of Senator Joseph McCarthy's Government Committee on Operations. One of the reasons he was chosen was to avoid accusations that the hearings were anti-Semitic. He also, like our current president, had a preference for secret meetings.

The problem for McCarthy—one that would soon destroy his career—was that Cohn wanted to bring along his boyfriend and nightclubbing buddy Gerard David ("G. David") Schine as the committee's "chief consultant."

Soon after McCarthy agreed, Cohn and Schine went on a "fact-finding" tour of Europe to look into whether U.S. libraries overseas carried any left-leaning books. It was unclear whether they rooted any Communist literature out of the library system, but the tour was a debacle, and an embarrassment to McCarthy. The honeymoon was over.

Shortly upon their return, Schine was drafted. Cohn convinced McCarthy to back him in a feud with the army. Hearings were held. Cohn resigned and went into private practice in New York. McCarthy remarked

---

* As of press time, David Dreier, the third of our role models, has not yet come out. Our basis for including him is, among other things, the lengthy article by Doug Ireland, "The Outing: David Dreier and his Straight Hypocrisy," *LA Weekly*, September 24–30, 2004.

that "putting a young man in charge of other men doesn't work out too well." He was censured and died two years later.

Back in New York, where Cohn grew up, he was much more at home, with clients such as Donald Trump, mafiosos John Gotti and Tony Salerno, and the Archdiocese of New York, and friends like Ronald and Nancy Reagan and Richard Nixon.

In 1984 he contracted AIDS, or, as he called it, "liver cancer." Two years later, he was disbarred from the New York Bar for unethical conduct and died the same year. He was buried wearing a tie with Ronald Reagan's name on it.

Antigay bona fides:

★ During Cohn's European "investigation," he blamed Samuel Reber, a State Department official in Germany, for an embarrassing press conference involving Cohn and Schine. According to his biographer Nicholas von Hoffman, in retaliation Cohn threatened to reveal a supposed homosexual relationship Reber had had as a Harvard undergraduate. Reber resigned.

★ Lester Hunt was a senator from Wyoming and a critic of McCarthy. While running for reelection, Hunt was told by either Cohn himself or Cohn's close friend Senator Styles Bridges, that unless Hunt dropped out of the race, it would be revealed that Hunt's son had been arrested for soliciting an undercover cop for "lewd and immoral purposes." Hunt withdrew from the race and, eleven days later, shot himself to death in his office with his hunting rifle.

★ Cohn campaigned heavily against New York City's first gay-rights ordinance, arguing that gays should not be allowed to teach in public schools.

Gay bona fides:

★ "Anyone who knows me and knows anything about the way I function . . . would have an awfully hard time reconciling, ah, ah, reconciling, that with ah, ah, any kind of homosexuality. Every facet of my personality, of my, ah, aggressiveness, of my toughness, of everything along those lines, is just totally, I suppose, incompatible, with anything like that," Cohn said to Ken Auletta in a 1970 interview.

* Cohn claimed to have at one time been engaged to longtime friend Barbara Walters.

* He sacrificed his career, and that of Senator Joseph McCarthy, to spend more time with his boyfriend G. David Schine.

* Cohn hung out a lot in gay bars after he returned to New York.

* He was known to be particularly fond of "muscle-boys."

*Ed Schrock*

Ed Schrock is a former Republican congressman from the Second District of Virginia, the home of Pat Robertson's Regent University and the Christian Broadcasting Network. Schrock had such strong conservative chops that he was chosen by his fellow congressmen to be the president of his incoming Republican freshman class in the Congress in 2001. The navy veteran (HELLO!) went on to serve on the House Armed Services Committee.

In the fall of 2004, Schrock decided not to seek a third term.

Antigay bona fides:

* Cosponsor of

    ☆ The Charitable Choice Bill, to allow churches and other religious groups that run social-service programs under Bush's faith-based initiative to discriminate in their hiring based on religion (i.e., you can refuse to hire gays because Jesus says they are sinners).

    ☆ The Federal Marriage Amendment, which says that "[M]arriage in the United States shall consist only of the union of a man and a woman. Neither this [C]onstitution [n]or the constitution of any state, nor state or federal law, shall be construed to require that marital status or the legal incidents thereof be conferred upon unmarried couples or groups."

★ His reelection platform in 2000 included reinstituting the ban on gays in the armed forces.

★ "You're in the showers with them, you're in the bunk room with them, you're in staterooms with them," Schrock told the *Virginian-Pilot* newspaper of Norfolk in 2000. "You just hope no harm would come by folks who are of that persuasion. It's a discipline thing."

Gay bona fides:

★ According to the Web site Blogactive.com, Schrock liked to hook up with other men using the MegaMates/MegaPhone Line, gay-dating/hookup service.*

★ Transcript of Schrock's personal ad:

I'd just like to get together with a guy from time to time just to—just to play. I'd like him to be, uh, in very good shape, flat stomach, good chest, good arms, well hung, cut, uh, just get naked, play, and see what happens, nothing real heavy duty, but just a fun time, go down on him, he can go down on me, and just, uh, take it from there. Hope to hear from you. Bye.

★ The gay magazine *Washington Blade* received six different audio tapes of Schrock leaving similar messages on the service.

### David Dreier

David Dreier is a twelve-term congressman representing the Twenty-sixth District of California. He is the chairman of the House Rules Committee, chairman of the California Republican House delegation, a former

---

* The actual audio is available for your enjoyment.

cochairman of Californians for Bush, and the former chairman of Arnold Schwarzenegger's transition team.

Antigay bona fides:

* A 92 percent approval rating from the Christian Coalition. Here are just a few of his votes that have no doubt contributed to the Christian Coalition's high opinion of Dreier:

  * 2004: Voted for the Marriage Protection Act.

  * 2001: Supported a law allowing federally funded charities to discriminate against gays and lesbians, even if that means overturning local laws.

  * 1999: Opposed the Employment Non-Discrimination Act.

  * 1998: Voted to prohibit gays and lesbians in Washington, D.C., from adopting children; opposed restoring funding for the Housing Opportunities for People with AIDS program.

  * 1997: Opposed the Hate Crimes Prevention Act; opposed increasing funding for state AIDS Drug Assistance Programs.

  * 1996: Voted for the Defense of Marriage Act; opposed the Housing Opportunities for People with AIDS program.

Gay bona fides:

* In Kitty Kelley's book about the Bush family, matriarch Barbara Bush is quoted as saying to a friend (regarding the fact that Dreier had dated her daughter Doro for a year and nothing had ever really happened): "[Dreier] never laid a hand on her."

* Dreier's chief of staff, Brad W. Smith, is also his roommate. Smith enjoys a salary of $156,600 a year (getting paid from Dreier's Rules Committee and by Dreier's office), which makes him the highest-paid chief to

any committee chair. This also turns out to be only $400 less than Karl Rove makes.*

★ In September of 2005, when Congressman Tom DeLay stepped down from his post as majority leader, the number-two leadership position in the House, Dreier was reported to be the first choice of Speaker Dennis Hastert to replace him. Conservative members, claiming Dreier was too "moderate," immediately revolted. The same day, Hastert selected Congressman Roy Blunt from Missouri, who was later replaced by John Boehner, neither of whom are rumored to be too moderate or gay.

---

* Like his boss and roommate David Dreier, Brad Smith has not confirmed that he is gay. Perhaps their unusual arrangement is simply because being that devoted to antigay legislation requires more time together than normal office hours allow.

# A QUESTION OF JUSTICE

It's clear that after years of complaining about liberal-activist judges, the Republican Party now stands as the true and sole flag-bearer of judicial accountability. The confirmation hearings of John Roberts and Samuel Alito before the Senate Judiciary Committee certainly were no exception. The Democrats asked ridiculous and superficial questions about "philosophy," "conflicts of interest," and the "law."

Those aren't things we need to know about judges. In a speech before the University of Tennessee College of Law in October of 2005, Senator Orrin Hatch lamented that Roberts had had to answer *over a hundred written questions* and sit through two "bruising" hearings before taking his lifetime seat.

Even then, before a single question had been asked in a hearing, Hatch was already happy with then-nominee Harriet Miers: "Personally, I will be satis-fied to learn that she will take a modest approach to the role of the unelected judges in our democracy." In fact, she was to take an extremely modest role, withdrawing her nomination three weeks later.

What it comes down to is that it's acceptable to *choose* a nominee based on ideology, but not to *confirm* on the same grounds. What kinds of questions *should* be asked in a hearing? As Hatch told the *New York Times*, "any member of the committee can ask whatever they want, no matter how stupid. But I don't think nominees have to answer certain questions. They don't have to answer questions about how they are going to vote in the future. They don't have to answer stupid questions. They don't have to answer argumentative cases."

So in the interest of expediting future hearings and never again forcing a nominee to answer "a hundred written questions," here is the list of Republican-approved questions for future Supreme Court nominees. Applicants may photocopy this form and send their answers to

*United States Senate Committee on the Judiciary*
*224 Dirksen Senate Office Building*
*Washington, DC 20510*

## PLEASE ANSWER THE FOLLOWING:

1. Do you believe that the Constitution protects the right of certain people to have things and to do stuff?

_____

_____

2. I've been having trouble shedding a few pounds around my thighs. I've tried everything—Atkins, South Beach, nothing works. To be honest with you, I just don't feel that comfortable around people with my shirt off. Do you have any advice?

_____

_____

3. How awesome are you?

_____

_____

4. The position you're applying for will require you to stay late some evenings or occasionally work weekends. Is this acceptable?

_____

5. Is law good?

_____

6. Do you support changing the level of our country's highest court from "Supreme" to "Extreme"?

_____

7. How'd you get so smart?

_____

_____

8. In the event we provide dinner, do you have any specific dietary restrictions we should be aware of?

_____

_____

9. You seem to have so much book learning and yet you're not all stuck up. How do you do it?

_____

_____

10. Do you have any questions for us about the position?

_____

_____

11. Do you think you could help my kid get into Princeton?

_____

_____

12. Some left-wing liberal crime apologists want to pass a law limiting the penalty for child rape to a simple written citation and stern lecture. In your educated legal opinion, would such a crime-loving law be right for our God-fearing country?

_____

_____

13. We know you can't be asked about how you'll rule on future cases, but do you, in fact, rule?

_____

14. Among the many things one could do from the bench, which of the following should you, in your legal opinion, *not* do from the bench:
   ☐ a) Order takeout
   ☐ b) Follow the Constitution
   ☐ c) Doodle
   ☐ d) Legislate

15. Let's say it's a Sunday night, it's 9 o'clock, and your TiVO is broken. You've got *The Sopranos* on HBO but *Law and Order* on ABC. What do you do?*

_____

_____

16. How soon can you start?

_____

_____

_____

* Actually, this is a hypothetical question and should have been removed. We regret the error.

# 14 · BUT WHAT ABOUT THE CHILDREN?

In April 2005, the Bush administration's Department of Health and Human Services created a Web site called 4parents.gov to help parents answer their kids' questions about sex. In addition to the advice about sex (tell your kids not to have it), the Web site also discusses how to talk to your child about sexual orientation:

> Sexual orientation is an issue that has become more visible in public debate, the media, and often, in school curriculum. As such, your child is certain to hear about alternative lifestyles at some point. Since adolescents are impressionable, parents need to address the issue of sexual orientation within the context of their own value system . . . If you believe your adolescent may be gay, or is experiencing difficulties with gender identity or sexual orientation issues, *consider seeing a family therapist who shares your values* to clarify and work through these issues.

Not that they're saying there's anything wrong with being gay—the therapist is just so you can "work through" it. But note, of course, that you should see a therapist that shares your values. And if you're prompted to see a therapist for this reason, we pretty much know what those values are.

Vigilant parents, however, know that the real battle is preventing your children from ever getting so confused that they might think they're gay in the first place . . .

☆ ☆ ☆

## SPONGEBOB SATANPANTS AND LENNY THE CROSS-DRESSING SHARK

Perhaps you heard that James Dobson of the fundamentalist right-wing group Focus on the Family had a problem with a cartoon character pushing "the gay agenda." But the person who first outed "SpongeBob" was a guy named Ed Vitagliano. He writes the culture reviews for the *American Family Association Journal*. Ed's review of the movie *Shark Tale* was titled "Something's Swishy About *Shark Tale*." And that something? That *Shark Tale* is a secret gay-converting machine in the guise of a children's movie. Ed had broken the code, the gay code. He broke it down one day for Sam, when Sam called him:*

**Ed:** *AFA Journal*, this is Ed.

**Sam:** Hi Ed, it's Sam Seder calling from the *Majority Report*. I just wanted to ask you some questions.

**Ed:** All right, that'd be fine.

---

* Edited for length and clarity.

**Sam:** Now, the gist of your piece was that there's an implicit homosexual agenda in *Shark Tale*?

**Ed:** *Shark Tale* carries with it a very obvious subtheme in which one of the main characters, Lenny, who's a shark, is obviously portraying and playing a role that is parallel to a homosexual teenager.

**Sam:** Okay. So what's the big tipoff that Lenny is secretly gay?

**Ed:** Lenny as a shark initially is shown to be a non-meat-eater and a disappointment to his father. His mannerisms in voice tend toward the effeminate. And he is an embarrassment to his father, and not only that, he likes to cross-dress, so to speak, as a dolphin, and is embarrassing to his macho father.* The son is different, fails to measure up to the cultural standards of manhood and this leads to rejection, and finally the father comes along and agrees to accept him anyway, as he is.

In today's climate, in which tolerance and diversity are being hammered in schools across the country, along with the message that we need to accept everybody just as they are, including gays and lesbians, it would not take long for children to begin to find in the back of their minds this message that it doesn't matter what a person's like or how he dresses, or how he acts, or what he likes in terms of relationships. I don't think it would take very long for kids to make that leap, which is the problem we saw with the movie.

**Sam:** That brings up another one, and this is something that I had a similar theory about—but I'd never seen it articulated the way you've done—is *Rudolph the Red-nosed Reindeer*, the version with the claymation. Do you know what I'm talking about?

---

* Okay Ed, we get it—you've got some issues with your really manly father.

**Ed:** Well, yeah I do. The only thing is that he very explicitly had a crush on a female deer. So, I think that—

**Sam:** I agree with that. But, see, I think the whole thing with him having a crush is a cover, because here you got a guy who's got literally, I mean, a flaming red nose.

**Ed:** Yeah.

**Sam:** And he wants to be a dentist, which is, you know—

**Ed:** Oh no, that was the elf that wanted to be the dentist—

**Sam:** Exactly! Okay, I mean that's my point, too. Those two hung around quite a bit. They were both—quote-unquote—misfits. And the elf in particular talked, I think, with a lisp.

**Ed:** Yeah, I probably wouldn't want to comment on Rudolph until, you know, I watched it again. It's just so hard to remember. I bet it's been fifteen or twenty years since I've seen it.

**Sam:** The guy couldn't play sports. He wouldn't play sports or, you know, reindeer games.

**Ed:** Yeah.


Now, granted, Ed wouldn't indict Rudolph—yet. Once he takes another look, he'll see that it's all just another cover for . . . tolerance. And for teaching kids that their parents will still love them—even if they're different.

* * *

## THE GOOD OL' DAYS

It's a slippery slope. But you won't find Dick Black on it. Dick is a member of the Virginia State House who wanted to ban gay people from being foster parents or adopting children in Virginia. He's convinced that it's better for children to remain orphans than be raised in a household that includes gay people, because, obviously, that might turn them gay. Black also cited what he believes to be a high incidence of suicide, child abuse, drug use, and depression among gay people. So it's not homophobia—it's just for the kids' own good.

The bill didn't pass, but in the hearings, another committee member, Senator Janet Howell, called Black on his concern for the children, and asked, does he then believe that all "depressed" people should be barred from adopting? "Yes," he responded.*

Black's star witness in the hearings was the "sociologist"† named Paul Cameron whom we last met describing homosexuality as like "pure heroin." Cameron added another objection: that gay people tend to die younger, at around fifty years of age. Where'd he get that number? From reading obituaries in the *Washington Blade*.

Given that there are so many reasons gays shouldn't be adopting, Sam called Black to get to the bottom of it.

After Black expressed his desire to keep children safe from gays, Sam asks:

**Sam:** Now, one of the things they'll say on the other hand is "what if you have a kid who is homosexual or who thinks he's homosexual or she thinks she's homosexual?"

---

* "Anti-gay Adoption Bill Killed," John M.R. Bull, *Daily Press* (Hampton Roads, Virginia), February 17, 2005.

† Cameron was booted from the American Psychological Association in 1983, and, three years later, in a sociologist smackdown, the American Sociological Association passed a resolution stating that Cameron was not a sociologist. Ibid.

**Dick:** Frankly, I don't think that happens. You know, what you have some-times, when you have young people, when you have teenagers, you know the homosexuals like to refer to them as being confused about their sexu-ality and this sort of thing. I don't think that's what it is. I think what happens is you have tension. Young men are nervous about interacting with women and young ladies are nervous about interacting with young men, and I think often the homosexuals step into that adolescent struggle that every one of us goes through, and they say "Hey, you really are homo-sexual." That's the reason that you're nervous about whether some boy is going to call you out for a date. And so, you need to just shift to someone of your own sex. And frankly, the media is so supportive of this very con-fused proposition.

**Sam:** How will they do that? Through direct mail?

**Dick:** I think it is principally something that comes out of Hollywood. It is the television and it's the movies.

**Sam:** And I guess prior to television and movies, it was . . . I guess radio, or . . .

**Dick:** Well, before television and the movies, we had frankly a pretty clean society. We didn't have this problem.

**Sam:** Right.

**Dick:** This is something that's relatively new.

**Sam:** Right . . . but how do you explain the homosexuals being around prior to the TV and the radio and the movies?

**Dick:** Well, here's the difference. They were always there just like they are there today. The difference is that as a culture we repressed that type of activity. That is the crucial element that is being lost in our culture today is we don't realize the importance of repressing this kind of activity.

**Sam:** Yeah, that's the thing, they don't wanna repress it. They wanna, you know, celebrate it and be normal.

**Dick:** Yes, and frankly, you know, I can have a degree of sympathy with someone who has this inclination and who gives into it so long as he's not doing it with the children. I can at least have some sympathy. The person I have no sympathy for is the person who then tries to foist that on everybody else and says, "Well look. This is correct. This is moral. This is just."

**Sam:** That's the problem—people trying to force their values onto the rest of us.

**Dick:** And they're certainly doing that in a very aggressive fashion.

**Sam:** Exactly. Well listen, I appreciate the conversation. And I wish you good luck in the next vote.

**Dick:** Wouldn't it be nice if the Senate of Virginia would have the same democratic principles as we're trying to instill in Iraq?

**Sam:** Exactly. Exactly. It'd be nice if we had a little bit more accountability all across the country.

**Dick:** I think that's true. Enjoyed talking with you.

**Sam:** Okay, bye.

**Dick:** Bye now.

# 15 · SO YOU WANNA BUY
# A CONGRESSMAN...

When you were younger, you never thought you'd feel old enough to get one. "Those are for old people," you thought. But now, suddenly, your twenties are behind you, maybe you're married, maybe you have a kid. Career's going fine, but now that it's finally all come together, you're feeling it's time to take the next step. It's time to buy a congressman.

And even if you don't feel that you're ready yet, you should be. There's never been a better time to pull the trigger. If you're a businessman, a small-business owner, or the leader of a corporation, a congressman is the latest must-have.

Let's face it, in a free-market economy, business is tough. And now that we no longer have a free-market economy, it's even tougher. It used to be that if you ran a good business, put out a good product, the marketplace would reward you. Well, times have changed, Methuselah!

You think a rising tide lifts all boats? Maybe so, maybe not. Right now it doesn't matter, because the Bush economy is no rising tide. Just ask GM and Ford, who were reduced to junk-bond status by Standard & Poor's in

May 2005. Or look at the fact that, as of April 2005, there were twenty-two thousand fewer jobs than when the Bush recession began in 2001. That $5.6 trillion surplus that existed when Bush took office?* It's now a $7.2 trillion deficit. Or the record 4.7 million bankruptcies that were declared in Bush's first term. Or that, as of May 2005, real wages were falling at their fastest rate in fourteen years. And how about the stock market? Like the Dow, you mean? The one that's down almost 50 percent from when Bush took office? At least it's not as bad as the NASDAQ, which is only about a thousand points, or 10 percent, below what it was when Bush was inaugurated.

No, it's clear that however free the free market was, those days are gone. The only real way to get ahead in business these days is to rig the system for yourself before someone does it against you. And the way you do that is by buying yourself a congressman. Look at it this way, all your competitors are doing it. You've got no choice.

Sure, it's daunting. There are 535 to choose from, and that's just incumbents. But when done right, owning a congressman can provide years of enjoyment.

Okay, you're thinking, I'm ready. But how to do it? Let *F.U.B.A.R.* show you, with our First Annual Consumer Report on Buying a Congressman.

☆ ☆ ☆

## RESEARCH, RESEARCH, RESEARCH

The models and varieties you have to choose from have never been better. But the first thing to remember is that being a happy congressman-owner means being an educated buyer.

There are many resources out there for you, especially on the Web. Sites like Political Money Line† and Common Cause track every donation to each congressman and to political action committees as well. These sites

---

* That was the surplus projected from 2002 to 2011.

† http://fecinfo.com/.

will give you a feel for the market, what the going rates are, what the most popular models are, and which of your competitors are buying.

★ ★ ★

## BUY OR LEASE?

A lot of people also ask, should I buy or lease? That's an easy decision, because with a congressman, it's the same thing. You "own" him or her until the next election, at which time, to continue getting the best use out of your congressman, you must make another payment. That's not to say you don't "own" the congressman—you do, he's yours—it's just that they prefer the payments be made on an installment plan.

★ ★ ★

## WHY DO YOU NEED A CONGRESSMAN?

The next thing to consider is: what will you be using your congressman for? To impress your friends? For a loophole for your business? Or maybe to deregulate your company's industry and be shielded from annoying and job-killing America-hating government regulators? To enact legislation that hampers your competition (who weren't smart enough to buy their own congressmen)? All great reasons, as the examples on pages 112–13 can attest.

★ ★ ★

## WHEN TO BUY?

Congressmen are in season all year round, though early in even-numbered years tends to be prime buying time. The smart buyer, however, can often pick up a bargain by buying during a political primary, sort of like buying straight from the factory. It's an obvious gamble. There is a benefit to being a congressman's first owner—to the extent that he/she can feel loyalty, the person in this position is most likely to be on the receiving end of it. But the differences between owning a near-congressman and an actual congressman are extremely large. It'll cost you more to wait, but at least you'll know whether what you've bought is a working congressman.

* * *

## NEW VS. USED

Like fine wines, congressmen become more valuable with age. Buying a first-termer isn't going to get you much, but it's not a bad starter-congressman. A ten- or twenty-termer is going to be a much richer experience, but it's really for the connoisseur.

* * *

## REFERRALS

Buying a congressman is not something you just jump into. It can be pricey, and, unfortunately, there is, as yet, no return policy. You can't even get House or Senate credit if you think you've bought a bum congressman. One way to minimize the risk is to talk to some of the congressman's past owners. Did they get what they thought they were paying for? Would they purchase one again? Would they recommend the congressman to their friends and colleagues?

* * *

## GO HOME

If the congressman you've got your eye on has been around for a while, one way to find out how right he'd be for you is to do some digging in his or her home district. Some prospective congressman-buyers don't know this, but congressmen actually have something called "constituents," which are people who live in the congressman's home district. It's possible some of these people are also owners of the congressman. For the most part, they're not but often make claims on the congressman as if they were.

## STYLE VS. SUBSTANCE

Don't make that first-time congressman-buyer mistake of going for flash over substance. If you're not buying a congressman for actual policy, then you're not ready to buy a congressman.

We've seen it a million times: the first-time buyers walking wide-eyed through the Capitol Hill showroom. They've come for a House member and their eyes are immediately caught by the senators.

Sure, senators are better looking, better dressed, more likely to have celebrity wives, but you need to ask yourself: do you really need a senator? Yes, they last longer between renewals (six years), but they're much more expensive. Plus, they're more likely to be major a-holes.

You don't buy a Lear jet to run down to the corner and pick up some milk, know what we mean? Eye on the prize. Eye on the prize.

\* \* \*

## DEAR GOD

While it's not foolproof, religion can be one indicator of whether you're going to be getting the most out of your congressman. It's not necessarily whether your congressman is religious, but *how* he or she is religious. Does the congressman belong to any religious or civil-liberties groups, like the ACLU? Does the congressman belong to any ecumenical groups? If so, you may want to keep looking.

If, on the other hand, your congressman is very overtly religious, makes a big deal of how religious he or she is, then you're probably looking at someone you can do business with.

★ ★ ★

## FINALIZING

While congressional purchases work in all sorts of ways, we can give you a tip to smooth the transaction. First, don't pay the congressman in cash. Even though it's not really different than paying in other ways (giving a check to the congressman's PAC, to the PAC of the congressman's party, or just a straight-out campaign contribution), it looks different—especially when captured on a grainy black-and-white surveillance tape. But the good news is there're no credit check and no waiting period. You write your check, boom, you're the proud owner of a shiny new congressman.

With proper upkeep, you can enjoy your congressman for years to come. Some people even say that their congressmen become almost like members of the family. Others treat theirs as actual human beings.

In any case, even if you don't have one yet, it's never too late. Get out there. They're waiting for you.

# A FEW SATISFIED CUSTOMERS

Meet Barry Myers, executive vice president of AccuWeather, a private company whose mission is "To save lives, protect property, and help people to prosper, while expanding AccuWeather as a healthy and profitable business."

Saving lives and making a profit. What a great company. The only problem was the National Weather Service was cutting in on that second part of AccuWeather's mission (and, actually, the first part, too). Basically, AccuWeather makes money selling weather data. But the damn National Weather Service was giving it away free. So Barry did what anybody who just wanted to save lives and expand a profitable business would—he found himself a congressman.

For what Barry needed, he thought a senator would be best. After some shopping around, he decided on Pennsylvania senator Rick Santorum, and gave him a $4,050 campaign contribution.

How'd it turn out? In April 2005, Santorum introduced a bill that bars federal weather services from competing with private companies . . . like AccuWeather.

Naturally, people who were used to getting that information for free aren't happy, like Scott Bradner of Harvard University. "I believe I've paid for that data once," said Scott. "I don't want to have to pay for it again."* As he understands the language of the bill, a huge portion of federal weather data would be prohibited from being accessed for free online.

To that, we say Scott should have bought his own congressman. Myers paid good money for his and he's simply using the congressman he rightly owns. Maybe Scott just isn't as interested in saving lives as Myers.

In fact, Myers says that the bill will force the National Weather Service to do less daily forecasting (which, after all, AccuWeather does just as well, for only a small fee), and devote more of its efforts

---

* "Feds Weather Information Could Go Dark," Robert B. King, *Palm Beach Post*, April 21, 2005.

to warning the public about tornadoes, hurricanes, and tsunamis.

Ed Johnson, director of strategic planning and policy for the National Weather Service, disagrees. "If someone claims that . . . [National Weather Service's] core mission is just warning the public of hazardous conditions, that's really impossible unless we forecast the weather all the time."

Of course, Johnson is just another disgruntled non-congressman-owner. Not such a "*strategic* planner," is he?

A lot of people think oil companies are raking in the cash. It's true, they are, but there's always more to rake in. Oil doesn't just jump out of the ground. You've got to find it first. And the more money you spend finding it, the less you have to spend on executive bonuses.

This is called "overhead." But what if you could get the government to pay for your overhead, so you could do other things with your huge profits, like keep them?

The energy industry knows a way: buy a congressman. And the congressman to have is Tom DeLay, from Texas. He'll give everything he's got, but he does require a lot of upkeep. That's why since 1984, the energy industry has given over $900,000 to DeLay's campaigns.

What'd they get? In April 2005, DeLay wrote into an energy bill a provision that would give a "research consortium" up to $200 million a year for ten years to "research" ways to take oil from the deep waters of the Gulf of Mexico. Once they find it, the oil is, of course, theirs to keep.

Naturally, a few tree huggers who don't understand how Congress works are upset by this.

Anna Aurilio, of something called the Public Interest Research Group, thinks it's just a way for the oil companies to make the payments they owe for drilling on federal land.

"This is really an end-run around paying their fair share," she said in the *New York Times*.* "These companies can and should do this on their own. They are laughing all the way to the bank."

So what? Maybe she should lighten up and buy her own congressman.

---

* "Energy Bill Includes $2 Billion Incentive for Gulf Drilling," Carl Hulse, *New York Times,* page 20.

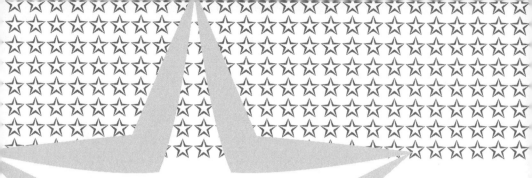

# 16 · HECK OF A JOB

But why stop there? If owning a governmental official is fun, just imagine how fun it is to *be* one. The good news, it's a lot easier than it used to be—if you're a crony of George Bush's, or a crony of one of his cronies. From 2000 to 2004, the number of jobs open to political appointees went up 15 percent, to 4,496, and the biggest growth within that number has been for jobs that don't need Senate confirmation.

Under Bill Clinton, these kinds of jobs fell by 5 percent, but President Bush showed resolve. His reasoning must have been: The terrorists hate democratic government, so I'll just make it bigger.*

According to Bloomberg News, not only is the number of political appointees growing, but they're also replacing career appointees, and going deeper into regulatory agencies. To take one example, from 2001 to 2004,

---

* Actually, we're just making that up. The reason he hasn't said it is probably just because he hasn't thought of that one yet. He'll get to it.

Bush's chief lawyer at the FDA was Daniel Troy, who replaced a career official. Troy needed no Senate confirmation, which is good, because his former job was representing drug and tobacco companies.

Of course, everyone knows the story of Michael "Brownie" Brown, the director of FEMA, whose incompetence created a third disaster for New Orleans, after Hurricane Katrina and the breaching of the levees, and failed Supreme Court candidate Harriet Miers, whom Bush nominated "because of our closeness."

If you want one of the 4,496 jobs and are thinking, "But I don't know Bush," don't worry. Brownie was actually a crony once removed, a tertiary crony, if you will. He got the job because he was a crony of Joe Allbaugh, who was a primary crony. Brownie and Allbaugh knew each other at Oklahoma State University, and after Allbaugh ran Bush's 2000 campaign, he got tapped as Bush's first head of FEMA. Then along came Brownie. Allbaugh, by the way, is now the head of the Allbaugh Company, a lobbying and consulting business whose clients include the KBR division of Halliburton. The company is currently enjoying a big contract to help "rebuild" New Orleans.

Oh, it was all shocking when the media shined the light on the dark side of the Bush administration for about fifteen minutes last fall. But, really, it's a perfect manifestation of George Bush. Who better not just to enjoy cronyism but, you know, really get into it than a guy who ran a failed congressional race based on his association with his father, failed at Arbusto, failed at Harken Energy, and wound up sitting on his hands for the Texas Rangers?

Bush may not be qualified to do his job, but he's qualified to appoint people who aren't qualified to do their jobs, who, in turn, appoint other people who aren't qualified. It's kind of a right-wing Republican twist on the old "teach a man to fish" axiom. Combined with the Amway growth model.

It used to be that crony jobs were in the backwater areas of government, like ambassador to Palau or something. Not anymore. You can take your crony ticket and go to the hot spots. Just look at Stewart Simonson, assistant secretary for public health and emergency preparedness, Department of Health and Human Services. This means he's responsible for "matters related to bioterrorism and other public health emergencies." Translation: the flu. Maybe even that avian flu! And before that? He got his job because he'd worked with HHS secretary Tommy Thompson when Thompson was governor of Wisconsin.

His background? He worked at Amtrak. This had led some critics to say that he's not qualified to coordinate our response to a flu pandemic, but if he can't help ensure we all get vaccines, his knowledge of mass transport will be handy when the mass chaos breaks out.

Then there's Julie Myers, the thirty-six-year-old new head of the U.S. Immigration and Customs Enforcement Division of the Department of Homeland Security. It's the largest investigative agency in the country next to the FBI. All she had to do was be a federal prosecutor in Brooklyn for a few years and bounce around Washington for a few after that. And also be the niece of former chairman of the Joint Chiefs of Staff General Richard Myers. Not even the Republican-run Senate would have confirmed her, so Bush had to use a recess appointment on January 4, 2006, to get her through.

Or Ellen Sauerbrey, another recess appointee. She's the assistant secretary of state for the Bureau of Population, Refugees and Migration, with a budget of $700 million. Sauerbrey has no experience with any of this, but she does have experience being a failed Republican candidate. This is a very good way to get a job in a Republican administration—they know failure, it's what bonds them, makes them feel close, it's what they do. Sauerbrey failed twice, both times to be governor of Maryland. After that she was a radio talk-show host, which, we'd like to say, we're in no way criticizing. Currently she's Bush's U.S. ambassador to the United Nations Commission on the Status of Women.

Our favorite, however, is Paul J. Bonicelli, who is the head of the democracy and governance programs for the United States Agency for International Development. This office plays a key role in Bush's plan to democratize the Middle East and get everyone there to stop trying to kill us. So maybe when he's traveling over there, he can tell them a bit more about himself. Like his former job as dean of a place called Patrick Henry

College in Purcellville, Virginia. And how the students there are required to sign a statement of belief that includes things like:

★ Jesus Christ, born of a virgin, is God come in the flesh

★ Jesus Christ literally rose from the dead

And this one, which must surely be very popular in the Middle East:

★ All who die outside of Christ shall be confined in conscious torment for eternity

In November 2005, Hawaii senator Daniel Akaka, senior member of the Senate Homeland Security and Governmental Affairs Committee, introduced a bill that would set down mandatory requirements for senior positions just in the Department of Homeland Security. But it's unlikely to impress the Bush administration. Clay Johnson III, who oversaw presidential appointments when Michael Brown was elevated to "Brownie," and is now the deputy director of the White House Office of Management and Budget, said the White House doesn't see the need for change. "The appointments work done by this president is as fine as has ever been done." Johnson was Bush's roommate at Yale (the "III" had to be a tip-off).

Bush has also pioneered a particular kind of crony appointment: he likes to take people who do have expertise—but in strictly political venues—and appoint them to policy-oriented positions. Karl Rove, to name just one example. And another, Karen Hughes, who is currently supplementing the fine work of Mr. Bonicelli. Here is her story.

★ ★ ★

## KAREN HUGHES: HURRICANE OF GOODWILL

As anybody who has lately been paying attention to the Middle East knows, our image over there has gotten a lot better. People seem to just, well, love us. And it's no accident. In the spring of 2005, longtime presidential aide Karen Hughes was sworn in as undersecretary of state for public diplomacy. As both she and her boss will tell you, it's a very important job—the United States' image in the Middle East has apparently taken a few hits in recent years.

According to the State Department, the position's responsibilities are to "ensure that public diplomacy (engaging, informing, and influencing key international audiences) is practiced in harmony with public affairs (outreach to Americans) and traditional diplomacy to advance U.S. interests and security and to provide the moral basis for U.S. leadership in the world." Or, in short, "to improve America's dialogue with the world."

And so seriously did Hughes take this responsibility that she only waited five months before deciding to start her job—yes, she wanted to wait for her son to go off to college before starting (it's well known that Middle Eastern America-haters tend to take the summer off anyway), but she did make the decision to go ahead and start before her son graduates in four years.

And Hughes's qualifications? Well, for starters, her George-given nicknames are "High Prophet," "the Enforcer," and "Hurricane Karen" (we don't know what level of hurricane but assume it's at least a "cat-four").

As her State Department bio states, she's also "an elder and longtime Sunday School teacher in the Presbyterian Church." And, according to her memoir, *Ten Minutes from Normal,* she once gave the sermon on Air Force One on Palm Sunday. Which she reprints in her memoir. In its entirety.

True, "High Prophet" doesn't speak Arabic or hold any degrees in foreign policy or Middle Eastern affairs, but she is a former TV news anchor—and is there anything more friendly than a TV news anchor?

President Bush expressed his confidence in Hughes at her swearing in:

We're in a war on terror. We are still at war. And to succeed in this war, we must effectively explain our policies and fundamental values to people around the world. This is an incredibly important mission. And so I've asked one of America's most talented communicators to take it on . . .

And why is it so important? Bush continued:

> In the war on terror, the world's civilized nations face a common enemy,
> an enemy that hates us, because of the values we hold in common.

Hughes, according to the other speaker that day, Condoleezza Rice, would reverse this, because of her ability "to show the world the true heart of America."

But it won't be easy. Because, Bush said:

> . . . our enemies use lies. They use lies to recruit and train and indoc-
> trinate. So Karen and her team have a vital task. They must ensure that
> the terrorist lies are challenged aggressively, and that our government is
> prepared to respond to false accusations and propaganda immediately.

Another reason why Hughes seemed like the perfect person was noted in Bush's conclusion:

> Finally, I've asked the State Department to encourage Americans to
> learn about the languages and cultures of the broader Middle East.

See that? Leading by example. Before she started, Hughes knew nothing about the Middle East nor its languages. So who better to help America learn this stuff? Hughes would learn *along with* us.

In her Senate confirmation testimony, "the Enforcer" typically broke it down so we could all understand it:

> I will be guided by four strategic pillars that I call the four "E's": engage-
> ment, exchanges, education, and empowerment.

That is a lot of E's. And it's hard to imagine anybody still hating us after so many E's.

She also said that she was "mindful that before we seek to be under-stood, we must first work to understand." And that's why her first act as our public ambassador was a "listening tour."

When explaining how she chose the countries she would visit, she showed off how much she had already learned about the region:

> You might want to know why the countries. Egypt is, of course, the most populous Arab country . . . Saudi Arabia is our second stop; it's obviously an important place in Islam and the keeper of its two holiest sites . . . Turkey is also a country that encompasses people of many different backgrounds and beliefs, and yet is proud of the saying that "All are Turks."

If you've ever been around Turks, you know how true that is. Hughes didn't list the exports and imports of each country, but you get the sense she probably could if she needed to.

Oddly enough, however, given all of this preparation—her qualifications, her communications talents, her four E's—the trip didn't go very well.

The tone was set on her way over, when she told reporters on the flight to Cairo, "I go as an official of the U.S. government, but I'm also a mom, a working mom." And to NBC News, "My most important job is Mom."

Okay, sure, a bit unexpected. A novel theory is that Hughes's love of being a mom would in some way stop people in the Middle East from hating us, but hey, maybe it'll work.

Or maybe not.

In Saudi Arabia, in front of a handpicked audience of five hundred women, she began with: "My most important title is that of Mom."

Which softened them up for her lecture on the importance of driving—tied in, of course, with the importance of being a mom.

> I feel as an American woman that my ability to drive is an important part of my freedom. It has allowed me to work during my career, it has allowed me to go to the grocery store and shop for my family, it allows me to go to the doctor. It gives me a measure, an important measure, of independence.

There's no denying those are handy things. But it didn't go over well with the Saudi women, who wanted Hughes to "listen" and "understand" and "learn" that they don't like being seen as victims by Americans. When one of them said, "The general image of the Arab woman is that she isn't happy. Well, we're all pretty happy," the crowd broke into applause.

As far as driving goes, in the opinion of Dr. Siddiqa Kamal, an obstetrician who runs her own hospital, "There is more male chauvinism in my profession in Europe and America than in my country . . . I don't want to drive a car. I worked hard for my medical degree. Why do I need a driver's license?"

It didn't go better in Cairo—where Hughes listed "the experience of having children and families" as one of the U.S. goals for the Palestinians.

And when asked about Bush's habit of talking about God in his foreign-policy speeches (or in all his speeches), Hughes replied that "many people around the world do not understand the important role that faith plays in Americans' lives." She also noted that "previous American presidents have also cited God, and that our Constitution cites 'one nation under God.' "

Perhaps Hughes was so busy being a working mom and loving—we mean really loving—children that she never took the time to read our Constitution and realize that the words "one nation under God" are found nowhere in it. Or maybe it was part of a clever campaign to win them over with humility—to say, see? I know as little about my own country as I do about yours! I'm all about equality. And I really love children. Can we talk about how we all love children?

At least she got it right when she said that President Bush was the first U.S. president to support a Palestinian state, right? Well, no, that was President Clinton. But she was correct that other presidents have also cited God.

On to Turkey, where Hughes's version of "engaging, informing, and influencing key international audiences" was to say: "I am a mom and I love kids. I love all kids. And I understand that is something I have in common with the Turkish people—that they love children."

That's the Turks. Always saying "All are Turks" and really loving children. Strangely, some of the Turks didn't want to talk about our mutual love for children. When one of them asked about the PKK, the armed separatist group based in northern Iraq, which some Turks believe the United States turns a blind eye to, Hughes said that it was "somewhat an irony," and that "sometimes you have to engage in combat in order to confront terrorists who want to kill you."

That didn't go over very well, either, as when one woman said to Hughes, "This war is really, really bringing your positive efforts to the level of zero." Of Hughes's appearance, the same woman later said she was "feeling myself wounded, feeling myself insulted here."

Even "High Prophet" herself seemed a bit down after the trip, declaring, "I think I did the best I could. I hope I'm an effective communicator."

We do, too, Karen. We believe in you.

So given the critical importance of your mission, we've decided to help you in what Bush calls your mission to "defeat them in the battle of ideas."

Here are a few ideas we've come up with, which seem up your alley and which we believe will be at least as effective as those of your first "listening tour":

### The Wheels of Understanding

A worldwide lottery for those not allowed to drive. The winner gets Undersecretary Hughes as their personal driver for one year. Plus you'll get to hear all her stories, including the ones left out of *Ten Minutes from Normal*—it's like two prizes in one.

### Trading Spouses: International Edition

Each week, every family in one country exchanges mothers with those of another country, as in the hit television show *Trading Spouses: Meet Your New Mommy*. Our worldwide love of being a mom is the one thing we all have in common. May as well start there.

### Middle Eastern Vacation

To further build on Hughes's goodwill, we send Clark and Ellen Griswold, from *National Lampoon's European Vacation*, for a tour of the Middle

East. You can't suicide-bomb somebody when you are laughing so hard at the Griswolds' side-splitting antics.

## *Hi*

Spend $5 million a year to produce a glossy Arab-English magazine about American life, targeted at Arab audiences.

Actually, they did do this one—but, sadly, *Hi* had to say "good-bye" after two years, shutting down in the fall of 2005. The last issue featured Texas as the "State of the Month."

## *Stop Killing Them*

A PR campaign whereby the United States stops killing them.

☆ ☆ ☆

## RON SILVER: ACTOR OF PEACE

In the fall of 2005, President Bush made a controversial appointment to a prestigious position, which some critics attacked—even before Senate hearings could be held—as the product of cronyism. Opponents claimed the person was appointed only as a reward for carrying water for President Bush.

We're talking, of course, about the appointment of Hollywood's Ron Silver to be a member of the Board of Directors of the United States Institute of Peace.

Now we know what you're thinking. "Wow, that sounds like a pretty important position. Is he qualified for that? I bet you guys are about to really let him have it." Well, as it happens, our friend and colleague Janeane Garofalo worked with Mr. Silver on TV's *West Wing,* where he played the delightfully unscrupulous Bruno Gianelli. With that said, if you know anything about Janeane—and all you have to do is listen to our radio show—it's important that we proceed . . . very carefully.

After giving the matter much thought, including what it's like when Janeane is unhappy with us, we've come to the conclusion that, yes, Ron Silver is actually very qualified.

Let us explain.

Yes, the USIP is an important organization. According to its Web site, it is an "independent, nonpartisan federal institution created by Congress to promote the prevention, management, and peaceful resolution of international conflicts." Its mandate is "to support the development, transmission, and use of knowledge to promote peace and curb violent international conflict."

In today's world, that seems like pretty important stuff. That's why the present board includes people like Dr. Holly Burkhalter, advocacy director of Physicians for Human Rights; Chester Crocker, former assistant secretary of state; and Seymour Lipset, professor of public policy at George Mason University.

They all seem to fall right in line with the law that requires board members to have "appropriate practical or academic experience in peace and conflict resolution."

This has led some naysayers to complain about Silver's qualifications and ask why a Hollywood actor would be appointed to this nonpartisan board, or qualified to do things like "identifying the best practices of conflict prevention, management, and reconciliation and of peaceful statecraft," and "training international affairs professionals from the United States and abroad in conflict prevention, management, and resolution techniques," and "organizing and supporting dialogues within and among parties to conflicts and providing technical assistance addressing emerging, ongoing, and recent disputes in areas of high priority to the United States."

These "blame America first" types point to the fact that the guy Silver would be replacing is Dr. Stephen Krasner, a Harvard-educated professor of political science at Stanford University who, according to his Stanford bio, specializes in "issues of market failure and distributional conflict in international political economy, and the historical practices of sovereignty especially with regard to domestic autonomy and non-intervention."

Though we're obviously not the biggest fans of President Bush, or of most of his appointments, we do occasionally make some money from Hollywood ourselves, and thus resent the implication that just because Silver is a Hollywood actor he's not an expert at international-conflict resolution, or would be less effective than a bunch of pointy-headed intellectuals just because they "know things."

Critics also claim that the appointment was just a cronyistic payback, because of the speech Silver gave at the Republican National Convention. And, yes, in that speech, Silver compared Bush to General MacArthur:

> At the end of World War II, General Douglas MacArthur, supreme allied commander of the South Pacific, said: "It is my earnest hope—indeed the hope of all mankind—that from this solemn occasion a better world shall emerge out of the blood and carnage of the past, a world found upon faith and understanding, a world dedicated to the dignity of man and the fulfillment of his most cherished wish for freedom, tolerance and justice."
>
> The hope he expressed then remains relevant today.

And, yes, Silver strongly endorsed the war in Iraq:

> We are again engaged in a war that will define the future of humankind. Responding to attacks on our soil, America has led a coalition of countries against extremists who want to destroy our way of life and our values.
>
> This is a war we did not seek.
>
> This is a war waged against us.
>
> This is a war to which we had to respond.

And, yes, Silver strongly endorsed Bush himself:

> Under the unwavering leadership of President Bush, the cause of freedom and democracy is being advanced by the courageous men and women serving in our Armed Services.
>
> The president is doing exactly the right thing.
>
> That is why we need this president at this time!

But if there's any evidence that speech was the reason why Bush appointed

Silver to replace Professor Krasner, we've yet to see a smoking gun. Plus, when asked by the *New York Times* whether this was an example of cronyism, Ron Silver certainly laid that question to rest: "No. 1, I am not a crony of the president. I have never been to Crawford." Q.E.D. Ron is clearly not a crony.

And while we agree with those who say we should "let the process work" and wait for the Senate hearings, we cannot let this canard against a fellow member of the Hollywood community stand.

Not only is there no evidence that this appointment was a quid pro war quo, there's abundant evidence that Silver was appointed because he's qualified. Don't believe us? Allow us to examine the facts. Silver has been working toward this moment his entire career. After we're done, you'll agree with us that the real scandal would be if Bush didn't appoint Silver to the United States Institute of Peace.

### Rhoda

Let's start with *Rhoda,* the sitcom, a spin-off of *The Mary Tyler Moore Show,* starring Valerie Harper. As most of you know, Rhoda Morgenstern was a sassy woman who grew up in the Bronx, fled for a time to Minneapolis (where she hung out with Mary Tyler Moore), and then moved back to her roots. As Rhoda said, "Now I'm back in Manhattan. New York, this is your last chance!"

You can feel the conflict welling up already. Throw in Rhoda's glum-but-zaftig sister Brenda, and it's practically a war. We bet Madeleine Albright never had to make peace with a couple of sisters like these, unlike Ron Silver, who came on in season three, playing Gary Levy, the swinging neighbor and "jean entrepreneur."

And take a look at episode seventy-six, "Lady's Choice," in which Brenda enjoys the luxury of having two boyfriends, Gary and Benny, competing for her attention until they both show up for a date on the same night.

The same night! You think that didn't require "identifying the best practices of conflict prevention, management, and reconciliation and of peaceful statecraft"? If you said no, clearly you've never been on a three-way date with Brenda Morgenstern!

## Silent Rage

Everybody knows that silent rage is the worst kind of rage, and this movie certainly shows that. You think the insurgents are tough? How about a psychotic superhuman killing machine created by scientists, which is terrorizing a small town? Oh, and did we mention kung fu? That's a solution that seldom gets brought up in international-conflict seminars—and that's because Ron Silver is still awaiting Senate confirmation.

True, it's not Ron Silver doing the kung fu—but that's only because Chuck Norris got the part of the street-fighting sheriff, and he's really good at it. But that doesn't mean that Silver couldn't take away from Sheriff Dan Stevens (Chuck Norris) that sometimes you have to bend the law and you can't always go by the rule book, like the suits downtown want. At least not with psychotic superhuman killing machines.

But Ron also learned a great deal from his own character, psychiatrist Dr. Tom Halman. A lot of people say that one of the problems right now in Iraq is that we don't understand what's fueling the insurgency, and why Al Qaeda is able to recruit so well. Well, Ron Silver could draw on his experience as Dr. Halman to "get inside the head" of these people.

This is how Silver would be able to "increase public understanding about . . . approaches to prevention [psychology], management [kung fu], and resolution [super kung fu]" of international conflict.

As one of the freaky scientists in *Silent Rage* says, "Nobody's going to give us a Nobel Prize for murder!" No, but they might for international-conflict management.

## Blue Steel

Silver gets even more perspective in this taut thriller—we know lots of thrillers get called that, but this one is really taut—starring Jamie Lee Curtis as rookie cop Megan Turner. She loses her gun, and the wealthy Eugene Hunt, played by Ron Silver, finds it. Eugene becomes obsessed with Megan and starts stalking her, even carving her name into bullets. Sounds like something high-ranking Al Qaeda officials would do, doesn't it? Well, Ron Silver has already done that, or at least played—and fiercely, at that— a guy who did that.

## Skin

We'll let Fox, the network that aired *Skin*, describe it for you:

> *Skin* is about sex and race. *Skin* is about politics. And, most of all, *Skin* is about skin: complexion, beauty, desire, attraction, obsession, and prejudice in contemporary Los Angeles. *Skin* is shot through with black comedy, passion, white-collar crime, scandal, naked ambition, and action.

Sound familiar? We'll make it easier for you. Read it like this, and you'll see how this series helped Ron Silver prepare for his new job:

> *International-conflict Resolution* is about sex and race. *International-conflict Resolution* is about politics. And, most of all, *International-conflict Resolution* is about skin: complexion, beauty, desire, attraction, obsession, and prejudice. *International-conflict Resolution* is shot through with black comedy, passion, white-collar crime, scandal, naked ambition, and action.

There you have it: not only is Ron Silver qualified to be our next representative at the United States Institute of Peace, it's the role of his life. This is no crony appointment. This is national security. Ron Silver, we give you two thumbs up.

# PROPOSAL: DEPARTMENT OF HOMELAND CRONYISM

If there's anything we can all agree on—actually, just about half the country seems to agree—it's that cronyism can be a bad thing. Sure it's easy to appoint a Brownie, but when they fuck up, it's incredibly expensive. It's fine to appoint a crony as the head of emergency preparedness, until the avian flu hits and it turns out rebuilding civilization is much harder than it would have been just to appoint someone who could get enough vaccines produced in time.

So we have a simple proposal that is truly a win-win—even for the Republicans: the Department of Homeland Cronyism.

Here's how it would work. The president appoints all his cronies to a new cabinet: old roommates, roommates of roommates, his baby-sitter, his accountant, his personal lawyer, an actor that made a speech for him one time. We—to use a Bush favorite phrase—smoke 'em out. It's like the "fly paper theory." It may not work in Iraq, but that's no reason it can't work here.

They'll be happier in the DHC anyway. First, they all kind of know each other. It'll be like a reunion: "I haven't seen you since that time on the quad! Hey everybody—this guy is *crazy!*"

And they can all have whatever title they want. Undersecretary of the Keg, or High Commissioner of Liquid Engineering, If You Know What I Mean, or Ambassador to Atlantic City. But here's the other key point: the department is fully funded—to the tune of hundreds of billions of dollars. Because that's *still* less than it would cost to fix their fuckups if they are allowed to muck around in real departments. So, all day long, they can just go around giving each other no-bid contracts, sweetheart deals, and inside information on their solid-gold phones.

Sure, we'd be allowing them to enrich themselves. But they're gonna do it anyway; the question is just how serious the consequences are gonna be for the rest of us.

That's called a win-win.

## 17 · WE HAVE NOTHING TO FEAR...But the People Outside My Administration Who Were Really Responsible for This

One thing you can say regardless of which party is running the government: when a catastrophe strikes one part of our nation, one big enough that it overwhelms local resources, the federal government steps right in. The swift use of the collective resources available only to the federal government serves as a fitting reminder that no matter where the trouble is, we're all one nation, and when one part of it is endangered, we're all endangered.

For example, just look at the response to Hurricane Katrina. It was a chance for President Bush to show us all what he was made of and what his vision of the country was. In fact, when such vision is called for, the Republicans and Bush often like to invoke FDR.

Indeed, the two came together during Katrina. The day after the levees in New Orleans broke, Bush was in San Diego, at the Coronado Naval Base, giving a speech to commemorate the sixtieth anniversary of V-J

Day. Bush noted the hurricane—"The federal, state and local governments are working side-by-side to do all we can to help people get back on their feet, and we have got a lot of work to do"—and then went right into the war on terror, using the legacy of his hero FDR:

> Franklin Roosevelt refused to accept that democracy was finished. His optimism reflected his belief that the enemy's will to power could not withstand our will to live in freedom. He told the American people that our liberty depended on the success of liberty in other lands. And he called on Americans to defend that liberty, and millions answered the call. Within four years, America would recover from the devastation of Pearl Harbor. Within four years, we would fight and win a world war on two fronts.

Some critics objected to Bush's comparison of himself to FDR, but that's just because they don't fully understand the role of the federal government the way George and Franklin do.

In fact, if you go back and read FDR's speech to the nation directly after the attack on Pearl Harbor, the similarity is obvious, and Bush's comparison is perfectly legitimate. Don't have it in front of you? We happen to have a copy right here.

## FRANKLIN DELANO ROOSEVELT'S SPEECH TO THE NATION

December 12, 1941

Five or six days ago, December 7, 1941—a date which will live in infamy—the United States of America was suddenly and deliberately attacked by naval and air forces of the Empire of Japan.

And I want to assure every citizen of this country that the federal government is going to have a very vigorous response to this situation.

I understand that some people are angry and frustrated. Frustration is a natural reaction when 441 fighter aircraft, 6 carriers, 2 battleships, 3 cruisers, and 9 destroyers attack you and kill 2,403 of you. But these things happen.

There are some, for instance, who have questioned why I am still at my home in Hyde Park, New York. And to those, let me say that I am no less involved in this situation from the second-floor terrace, where I am speaking to you now, than I would be at the White House.

When the White House was informed of this attack on December 9, it was our understanding that the worst of it was over.

Some have asked why air support was not called in to try to minimize the damage from the attack, or why other battleships in the area have still not been mobilized, or why a declaration of war has not been made.

I share this frustration. Please understand that the federal government is a large operation, and there is a lot of paperwork involved in these things.

What's more, the federal government works best when it is assisting the efforts of local and state government. Accordingly, we are being careful not to hinder the work of Honolulu mayor Lester Petrie, who is the local official with primary authority over Pearl Harbor.

Though I by no means wish to cast aspersions on Mayor Petrie, when the attack started, we were waiting on a request for help from Mayor Petrie. Yes, it's true, we have several hundred fighter planes stationed at nearby H        man Air Force Base, ready to go. But until we received a for             t for them from the mayor, our hands were tied.

So   e      our critics, those who are always ready to blame America first, say that we should mobilize the federal troops, for instance, the United States Army, Air Force, Navy, and Marines, and avenge this attack on Pearl Harbor.

Let me say that we are considering all options, but we, of course, want to be careful to let Hawaii governor Joseph Poindexter take the lead in this matter. It was his state, after all, where the attack occurred, so he naturally bears primary responsibility for all aspects of it.

As for how the attack occurred in the first place, I want to say that now is not the time to play the "blame game." Admiral Husband Kimmel, commander in chief of the Pacific Fleet, and Lieutenant General Walter Short, commander of all U.S. military installations on

Hawaii, did a heck of a job in making sure we were prepared for such an attack.

The truth is, it wasn't until an hour or so into the ninety-minute attack that it was generally known that this was, in fact, an attack, and not just a few sightseeing planes enjoying what is, by the way, a spectacular view over one of our finest ports—I encourage anyone who can to take one of those sometime. It's a great experience for the entire family.

Though, of course, our hearts go out to the loved ones of those killed in the attack, there is very little the federal government can do when people choose to steer their ships directly into the path of an attack. When the relationship between Japan and the United States began to become acrimonious, and the possibility of hostilities became more ominous, the federal government issued a warning asking people to please stay out of the path of an attack.

Though I'm not here to single any person out, we did request that Mayor Petrie and Governor Poindexter issue mandatory orders for people to avoid being attacked by the Imperial Japanese Army, but those calls went unheeded.

But again, I'm not here to get involved in a "blame game" or even a "he said she said." What's done is done, and we need to work together to rebuild Pearl Harbor. I myself have many fond memories of some . . . "youthful" times on spring break in Pearl Harbor. In fact, I'll tell you this, Sunday wasn't the first time someone got bombed in Pearl Harbor [laughter].

And that's why we're going to make the new Pearl Harbor bigger and better than ever. And America is going to be a stronger country for it. Out of the rubble of Mayor Petrie's house—he's lost his entire house—there's going to be a fantastic house. And I'm looking forward to sitting on the porch.

To those who are calling for revenge against the Japanese for this dastardly attack, we hear you. The private sector is responding and showing that true American spirit of individual enterprise.

That's why I'd like to encourage all Americans who felt moved by the attacks to do what they can. Government action is one thing, but there's nothing more American than that private-sector, volunteer can-do spirit. Already people from all over the country are donating ammunition and homemade flying machines, and children are sending in their fireworks and sparklers.

So, to all Americans, I say go purchase a gun, maybe join a private militia, then make your way somehow over to Germany and Japan and show them that the individual private-sector initiative that they hate so much and tried to attack isn't dead here in America. Not by a long shot. And know that you'll have the full support of the federal government—and myself—here behind you, should you, in fact, make it back here.

Hostilities exist. There is no blinking at the fact that our people, our territory, and our interests are in grave danger. Now get out there and show the world what America really stands for.

# 18 · THE MEDIA IS NOT YOUR FRIEND

## PART ONE: ADAM NAGOURNEY

Fox News is horrible! What a bunch of right-wing phonies! Ooh they make me so mad.

Yes, yes, it's true. And chances are, you already know this. In fact, everyone knows this. Which means that everyone values the information coming out of Fox accordingly. Everyone's currency translation algorithm (aka "bullshit detector") for Fox News is more or less accurately calibrated.

So, no (with apologies to a colleague of ours named Al), Fox News is not a problem. But that certainly doesn't mean the media is your friend. Because it's not. In fact, that's one of the main reasons why the nightmare was allowed to happen in the first place. The media is one of the few entities that had the power to stop it. So why didn't it?

We're going to show you how, in this very long and exhaustive section of media criticism.

Just kidding. There are few phrases more frightening than "media criticism." We apologize to those of you whose foreheads may have just hit the
table at the very mention of it.

Actually, we don't need to look at the entire media, because we have a
perfect microcosm in a reporter named Adam Nagourney, the chief political correspondent of the *New York Times*.

*(Note from Stephen: Nothing agitates Sam more than Adam Nagourney. And,
oddly, nothing soothes me more than seeing Sam agitated. So I hereby yield
the page to one Sam Seder.)*

Full disclosure: nothing agitates me more than *New York Times* chief
political correspondent Adam Nagourney. If you want to see why the so-
called liberal media is, in fact, not liberal, Adam Nagourney is your guy.
Let's look, specifically, at how Adam covered the 2004 presidential race.

Why bother with Nagourney? Because he's not just in the media—he's
at the *New York Times*. And for better or worse (worse), the "take" of the
*New York Times* goes a long way to shaping the "take" of the entire media.
The *Times* has a lot of clout—and the *Times* takes a lot of pride in this and
gets a lot of mileage out of it. But how responsibly does the *Times* use this
clout? Meet Adam Nagourney.

One of the things the media loves to do is "get inside" the candidate's
head. The media loves to report on politics through the prism of personality. So, since that's fair game, let's get inside the head of the *Times* for a
moment. (Warning: What's going on in there isn't pretty.)

The *Times* knows that the right wing considers the *Times*'s coverage to
be "liberal." This is deeply wounding to the *Times,* and they'll do almost
anything to counter it. The method they've chosen for this is the idea of
"balance." Balance is their paramount virtue.

What this means in practice is this: Every Issue Has Two Sides And
They Must Be Presented Equally. All The Time.

No conclusions can be drawn by the reporter. When any fact that is
generally considered true by the culture is challenged, it is immediately
taken off the table of General Assumed Knowledge and put in a different

category, the category of Things We Can Never Really Know. All it takes is one person to make this challenge. And when that happens, the *Times* sees its job as simply to present "both sides."

For instance: "Republicans today announced that there is no such thing as gravity. Meanwhile, Democrats claim that there is such a thing as gravity. One thing is certain, though—this controversy is not going away any time soon."

And that's that. You're left to determine the validity of each side's contention. In the case of gravity, most of us (a diminishing number, if you read the news about various school boards across the country) know that the Republicans' claim is untrue (a word the *Times* doesn't like to use very much).

One might assume that the news outlet would give the reader some context, like pointing out that, in fact, there is near-universal acceptance of gravity. In the absence of that information, we assume that there isn't such universal acceptance, and "opinion is divided."

At the *Times*, the truth is always—*always*—in the middle. Both sides are always equally guilty/credible/cynical. Why? Because to say otherwise might confirm the long-standing canard that the *Times* is liberal.

The conservatives' campaign to define objectivity as "liberal" has been a stunning success (which explains a lot about the current administration). The *Times* has not only bought into this, but has deeply internalized it. The *Times* seems to think that objectivity and balance are somehow compatible—and not actually antithetical.

So, now, imagine all this swimming in the head of a *Times* reporter. And imagine how it's all compounded, because the reporter in question is actually liberal. Further imagine how this makes the reporter very nervous, afraid that he might be attacked for being liberal.

Now imagine that the reporter works at a newspaper that routinely gets attacked for being liberal, and vehemently denies it—a paper that makes it clear that nothing is to appear in its news coverage that would lend credibility to such attacks. Such a reporter would reasonably think his career trajectory at the paper would be hurt if his coverage attracted such attacks.

So what's the path of least resistance for such a reporter? How does he make sure he's not even close to drawing such attacks? He simply over-compensates, making sure to always err on giving the Republican side as much latitude and credibility as he can.

You have just imagined Adam Nagourney.

I spent many a night on the *Majority Report* attacking Nagourney for two reasons. First, the easy one: his reporting of the 2004 campaign was almost comically biased toward George Bush. Second, in the course of inter-viewing other journalists on the *Majority Report*, I heard many stories of how easily intimidated many of their colleagues were by right-wing e-mail and phone-call campaigns critical of their reporting.

One journalist told me, "What happens when you get three thousand e-mails from conservative zealots is that you'll think twice before you report that the world is round."

So reporters see the clear disincentive of looking critically at conserva-tive claims. No one wants to sit down and write a piece that they fear will shut down their e-mail for a day. It's easier not to bother. Just get the piece done. Doesn't have to be true—that might cause trouble. It just has to be satisfactory. Fly under the radar. Advance up the ladder.

This is why the fact that many reporters lean liberal in their personal views ends up being such a boon to conservatives. Nagourney and the *Times* have a much more pernicious effect on the system than Fox News. The result is that you have conservative media doing conservative reporting, and so-called liberal media doing . . . conservative reporting.

Obviously, we're not going to change the way the *Times* reports on poli-tics, but we're hoping that our little media vendetta against Adam Nagour-ney can at least get you to be a little more skeptical of the *Times* political reporting, to simply see the *Times* for what they are, in the same way most people see Fox for what they are.

### The Editor Made Me Do It

On May 27, 2004, a piece appeared in the *New York Times* with the fol-lowing headline and byline: "Democrats Wonder if Kerry Should Stay on Careful Path," by Adam Nagourney.

In and of itself, the headline does not seem unreasonable. It expresses Democratic doubt in Kerry's campaign tactics and suggests that he should be bolder.

But the next day, May 28, a blogger nicknamed SWOPA, posting on needlenose.com, decided to put Nagourney in a bit of context. What he did was post a collection of the headlines from Adam Nagourney's pieces over the course of the entire campaign. When viewed this way, a pattern began to emerge:

MARCH 19, 2003
"DIVIDED DEMOCRATS CONCERNED ABOUT 2004,"
by Adam Nagourney

APRIL 16, 2003
"LOOKING AT POSTWAR BUSH, GLUM DEMOCRATS PONDER
HOW TO WIN IN 2004," by Adam Nagourney

MAY 4, 2003
"LISTEN UP, DEMOCRATS: WHY 2004 ISN'T 1992,"
by Adam Nagourney

MAY 4, 2003
"DEMOCRATS' FIRST PRESIDENTIAL
DEBATE SHOWS PARTY FISSURES,"
by Adam Nagourney

MAY 17, 2003
"KERRY INTRODUCES HEALTH PLAN, POINTING UP DIVISIONS
AMONG DEMOCRATIC CONTENDERS," by Adam Nagourney

MAY 25, 2003
"THE DEMOCRATS ARE RUNNING, BUT WHO'S WATCHING?"
by Adam Nagourney

JUNE 15, 2003
"A FUND-RAISING SPRINT BY BUSH
WILL PUT HIS RIVALS FAR BEHIND,"
by Richard W. Stevenson and Adam Nagourney

JULY 9, 2003
"TRICKY QUESTION FOR DEMOCRATS: WHEN IS OPEN SEASON
ON ONE ANOTHER?" by Adam Nagourney

JULY 18, 2003
"POLITICAL MEMO; TUG OF CONSTITUENCIES STRAINS DEMOCRATS,"
by Adam Nagourney

JULY 29, 2003
"CENTRIST DEMOCRATS WARN PARTY NOT TO PRESENT ITSELF
AS 'FAR LEFT,'" by Adam Nagourney

AUGUST 31, 2003
"WORRIED DEMOCRATS SEE DAUNTING '04 HURDLES,"
by Adam Nagourney

DECEMBER 10, 2003
"DEMOCRATS WRESTLE WITH THE GORE FACTOR,"
by Adam Nagourney and Edward Wyatt

DECEMBER 18, 2003
"CANDIDATES IN PRESIDENTIAL CONTEST ARE FAILING
TO MOVE DEMOCRATIC PRIMARY VOTERS, POLL SHOWS,"
by Adam Nagourney and Janet Elder

DECEMBER 29, 2003
"STUMPING GAMELY, THE DEMOCRATS FIGHT AGAINST MOST
VOTERS' HOLIDAY INDIFFERENCE," by Adam Nagourney

JANUARY 1, 2004
"DEMOCRATS' PLAN FOR EARLY NOMINEE MAY BE COSTLY,"
by Adam Nagourney

JANUARY 9, 2004
"IOWA; TIDE OF SECOND THOUGHTS RISES AMONG DEMOCRATS,"
by Adam Nagourney and Carl Hulse

After Kerry clinched the nomination, even Nagourney had to note it, as he did with the following two pieces:

JANUARY 29, 2004
"PARTY LEADERS EXPRESS RELIEF AT THE EMERGENCE OF KERRY,"
by Adam Nagourney

FEBRUARY 9, 2004
"DEMOCRATS SEE UNIFIED PARTY FOR NOVEMBER,"
by Adam Nagourney

But then it was back to the business of being "balanced":

MARCH 13, 2004
"POLITICAL MEMO; TESTING, TESTING. SHREWD POLITICS OR
KERRY FOOT-IN-MOUTH SYNDROME?" by Adam Nagourney

MARCH 21, 2004
"POLITICAL MEMO; SOME DEMOCRATS SAY KERRY MUST GET BACK
ON THE TRAIL," by David M. Halbfinger and Adam Nagourney

APRIL 1, 2004
"POLITICAL MEMO; BAD TIMING AS KERRY SLIPS OUT OF PICTURE,"
by Adam Nagourney and Jodi Wilgoren

APRIL 8, 2004
"BATTLES IN IRAQ BRING PROBLEMS FOR
BUSH AND KERRY AS WELL,"
by Adam Nagourney and Carl Hulse


MAY 2, 2004
"KERRY STRUGGLING TO FIND A THEME, DEMOCRATS FEAR,"
by Adam Nagourney


MAY 27, 2004
"DEMOCRATS WONDER IF KERRY SHOULD STAY ON CAREFUL PATH,"
by Adam Nagourney


Apparently, the Democrats are weak and divided and Kerry is a real loser.

Well, Kerry *did* lose, right? Yes, he did. But who knows what would have happened had Nagourney told the truth? The idea of seeming to be a "winner" or seeming to be a "loser" is incredibly important in a presidential race. The exact same campaign speeches, gestures, commercials can seem desperate or confident, depending upon how the candidate has been framed by the media. And how the media frames a candidate is due in no small part to how the *Times* frames a candidate. If the *Times* says you're a loser, you get regarded as a loser, and it becomes a self-fulfilling prophecy. And then Adam can just pat himself on the back: I knew it all along.


*Charisma*
But just how far would Adam go to show that, no sir, he's no liberal! Exactly how skewed was Adam's perspective on the man he was covering?

On July 6, 2004, Nagourney was on *Charlie Rose* to discuss John Kerry's pick of John Edwards to be his running mate. Was there a danger Edwards would overshadow John Kerry? Charlie asked.

Adam's reply: "Hey, I could overshadow John Kerry!"

This from a man whose high salary is presumably for his observational prowess. At the very least, it's safe to say Mr. Nagourney's view of himself is no less deluded than his view of John Kerry.

> **John Kerry's height in ft.: 6' 4"** | **Adam Nagourney's height in ft.: 5' 6"\***
> **Number of Purple Hearts: Kerry: 3** | **Adam: 0.**

After this aired, we invited Nagourney to come on our show and demonstrate his "overshadowing" prowess for our listeners, but he never accepted.

So why does Adam do it? Well, this probably explains it: a colleague of his, with whom I spoke at the DNC, says that Nagourney didn't personally dislike Kerry and isn't actually conservative. Nagourney is also the coauthor of *Out for Good: The Struggle to Build a Gay Civil Rights Movement in America,* and happens to be gay.

When you write a book like that, you might assume that people might assume you're kind of liberal. So to "balance the scales," you look for any information in any story that can "give context to" the conservative side. You withhold skepticism about anything the conservatives say, because not plugging their "side" in the story would leave it too lopsided. And once you've presented "both sides," you definitely refuse to draw any conclusions. Never ever do that. Unless that conclusion is: "[Democratic candidate's name] is weak."

★ ★ ★

## PART TWO: TOM FRIEDMAN THROUGH THE AGES

"Things can't be as bad as you guys say, because every time I read Tom Friedman, everything just seems, well, better." That's a common reaction.

---

\* We couldn't find out Adam's exact height. But in the October 22, 2003, edition of the *New Republic,* Michael Crowley reports that Howard Dean, responding to a piece in the *New York Times* in which Nagourney called Dean "diminutive," noted that Nagourney is "about five-three." Because Dean was probably just ball-parking, and to make it more of a contest, we're giving Adam three more inches.

What you have to understand is that when Tom is writing about Iraq, or India, or the Middle East, what he's really writing about is Tom Friedman. Specifically, Tom Friedman's incredible ability to just feel so darn sunny about things. Not only is Tom just, doggonit, an optimist, the implication is that your failure to see what Tom sees means that you're a "pessimist," or a "cynic," or somebody who "wants America to fail." What's important isn't the facts about a situation but, rather, how you "feel" about the situation. And whether you're brave enough to call it like it is.

Fortunately, Tom is traveling the world, using his powers of empathy and description to put you right there in the situation. You might even meet a few real people. With real names. Through the specifics of their story, he will show the way. This is his shtick. His thing. It's what he does.

Why does any of this matter? It matters because Tom Friedman is the chief foreign-relations columnist for the *New York Times*. Hard to believe, but what he says actually carries weight. And in the last three years, it turns out that Friedman's shtick overlapped perfectly with Bush's need for intellectual cover for the war in Iraq. It was a win-win situation. Bush got some badly needed credibility on what some people still take to be "the left," and Friedman got to be the gutsy truth-teller, going against his own side of the spectrum, because, darn it, the love of his country was just a higher calling than that of the narrow, cynical, partisan, quasi-traitors whose skepticism about Iraq was really just a mask for cheap political gain at the expense of our country and our troops.

How would Tom have covered other events down through the ages? Well, as it turns out, so great is Tom's sunny optimism that it has actually triumphed over mortality itself. Aging and death are for partisan cynics—not Tom Friedman. And here's the proof: recently unearthed Tom Friedman columns (the raw goodness of his soul flowed right from the pen onto the paper and kept them from decomposing), going all the way back to the Roman Empire. Cynics beware—read slowly; going too fast may actually blind you.

## WHO'S AFRAID OF GLOBALIZATION?

(August 21, 410 A.D.) THE ALPS—I was at a dinner party last night with some friends and was struck by their pessimism. Yes, Alaric and the Visigoths have overrun the entire peninsula, yes, they've sacked Rome, and yes, they have flayed and burned most of the relatives of the guests at the dinner, and yes the entire city is on fire, and yes they're slaughtering and raping the remaining inhabitants.

Call me a cockeyed optimist, but I think this might be the best thing to ever happen to Rome.

"What?" I bet you're wondering. "Hey, Tom, how could you say such a thing? That is the opposite of what most people are thinking! We are threatened by your courage to hold this opinion! It is so strange, we don't understand it! It must therefore be brilliant! Could you explain it to us?"

If that's not what you're thinking, you are probably so hidebound in your pessimism and conventional thinking and failure to see the big picture, it is what you should be thinking. And so, yes, I will explain it to you.

Under Flavius Honorius, we Romans had grown lazy and complacent. Our lack of being beaten and raped and killed and enslaved had made us complacent.

As I was leaving the city for my remote mountain hideaway—I decided that it was important that someone be able to chronicle the healthy changes that are happening, and so I have reluctantly accepted the sacrifice of not being able to experience the excitement of going through these thrilling innovations with you firsthand—I saw the Visigoths pouring in. I went up to one, a young man named Athanaric.

Some of our leaders seem too afraid of these marauders, but that's just because their limited minds won't let them see the possibilities, so they try to keep the new ideas of the Visigoths at bay.

Take Athanaric, for example. He is a sturdy young man, full of promise, eager for new things, boundless energy. He was hungry for experience, and ready to work for it. For example, when I went up to talk to him, he grunted, decapitated my driver, and set about eating my driver's leg.

That's the kind of hunger Rome needs. He saw a need—to fill his stomach—and he efficiently filled it, with my driver's leg. And he did it without a lot of debate, and guild rules, and talk of "the rule of law" and "vacation time."

We Romans were overly contented with such things. Ample housing, jobs, nonslaughtered family members, intact legs—these are things we took for granted.

That's why I continue to be optimistic about how positive this will be for those Romans who somehow manage to escape being enslaved or slaughtered, their brutalized bodies paraded through the city and their severed heads mounted upon pikes for all to see.

One of the great things about extreme deprivation is that it awakens the senses. When most everyone you know has been killed, it makes you glad to be alive.

That's why we should reject the pessimists—those that remain alive, anyway—who have been fighting this healthy globalization. Far from fighting off the Barbarian Hordes from the North, we should look at the sacking of Rome as positive change, just another stage of life—or nonlife, depending on how quickly you were able to flee the city.

Out of adversity, and other people's deaths, will come benefits for the rest of us, or at least the few that were smart enough to reach the Alps before the serious raping and slaughtering began.

## THE WORLD IS FLAT

(June 21, 1633) VATICAN, ROME—I was standing in St. Peter's Square, and I started talking to a delightful eight-year-old little urchin. He looked up at me and, with the optimism, good cheer, and hopefulness that only a person who will likely be dead in one or two years can summon, said: "Galileo should die!"

Now, I know it's not always wise to be making important state-policy decisions based on the random blurtings of an anonymous peasant imp but, in this case, as in most cases, it is.

Much has been written about the current impasse between Pope Urban VIII and the astronomer Galileo Galilei.

In his *Dialogue Concerning the Two Chief World Systems,* Galileo presents two theories of the makeup of the universe: the heliocentric and the geocentric. And now the Holy See is about to put Galileo on trial in front of the Roman Inquisition.

It reminds me of a conversation I had recently with a local farmer while I was traveling in Tuscany with my son, Ethan, my daughter, Ashley, and our nine slaves. When our caravan approached, the lout was crossing the road with his oxen. I immediately took the opportunity to have a word with the roughneck.

As I jumped down and began to flog the hayseed mercilessly, I noticed a sextant fall out of the rowdy's tattered rags. I was fascinated. Here was a simple cretin, not a single tooth in his head, likely illiterate, and yet the lubber had this sophisticated piece of scientific equipment. I interrupted my son, to whom I had given the whip (this was to be a learning vacation, after all), and asked the churl, "Excuse me, yob, what exactly do you do with this gadget here?"

The dullard looked up at me and said, "I don't know. I just found it."

I thought to myself, smiled, kicked the ragamuffin into some swine dung, and we carried on. But the guttersnipe had a point.

"I don't know." Could anything more eloquent be said about our present dilemma in Rome?

Here we are, coming up on the middle of the seventeenth century, with ten cardinals about to try Galileo for saying the Earth revolves around the sun, and an excrement-covered scapegrace *campesino* has inadvertently provided the answer: science.

If the Western world is to move forward from this predicament, Galileo and the Church will have to be reconciled, and, as always, technology is the solution.

But not just any technology. We need to make use of the most advanced and innovative thinking and techniques available.

For instance, yes, the Iron Maiden of Nuremberg is a forward-thinking piece of machinery, with tomblike interior covered with spikes so that, when closed, they do penetrate the heretic's arms and legs and buttocks in several places, but not enough to kill him.

But there are new, even more scientific methods available. When I was visiting Spain recently, I saw that they were having great success with the Rectal Pear, a metal contraption forced into the rectum and expanded by the use of screws until the segments, at their widest aperture, mutilate their host irredeemably.

The Roman Inquisition has been resistant to the use of technologies from the Spanish Inquisition, but if Galileo is going to be forced to abjure, curse, and detest his heliocentric theories, Pope Urban VIII is going to have to break down these barriers that are hampering and stifling competition.

In France, I saw a fascinating device called the Shin Vice. It's simply an iron press with small bumps on the inside of the cuff, which cause intolerable pain when the device is pressed around the leg. It's much cheaper than the Iron Maiden, and doesn't require nearly as many torturers as the Rack or the Judas Cradle, in which the heretic is lowered on chains onto the point of a pyramid until his or her weight fully rests on the vagina, the anus, or the scrotum. This is very effective, but a country that requires five men to gain a heretic's confession will never be able to compete in God's eyes with one that requires only one to do the same job.

To move forward, a society can never stop innovating. And the society that does this best is going to be the one that proves to Galileo that it is the sun that revolves around the Earth, and that the world is flat.

That's the way the world is, and any society that doesn't realize this is going to be kicked into the ditch in a big pile of swine dung.

## THE GUN OR THE PEACE PIPE?

(December 30, 1890) WOUNDED KNEE CREEK, NEAR PINE RIDGE INDIAN RESERVATION, SOUTH DAKOTA—In my swing out to the western territories, I am now convinced more than ever that there is a solution to the Indian problem. And here it is: the Indians themselves.

Because, despite all the shameful blunders committed by United States generals and presidents, at the end of the day, the Indian nation is going to be what the Indians decide to make of it.

The Indians, or at least what is left of them, need to decide for themselves what kind of nation they are going to be. Yes, U.S. forces have made mistakes. As I've said in earlier columns, I thought the Indian Removal Act was too unilateral and didn't include enough job incentives, and I've raised questions in the past about the sometimes negative effect of wholesale slaughter on our negotiations with the Indians. Democracy building is hard work, though I still believe our decision to go into the Indian lands and bring them freedom was the right thing to do.

But we can't do it alone. It's 1890 now. We've been trying to build an Indian democracy for a hundred years. We've even given the Indians their own department in the government: the Office of Indian Affairs. So now it's gut-check time for the Indians—again, at least for those whose guts are still intact enough for them to check—do they want to finally join the process, or do they want to continue to play the blame game about who stole whose land, who mass-slaughtered whom, who assassinated whose political and spiritual leaders?

Are the Indians willing, at long last, to take "yes" for an answer? Do they want to embrace the past or embrace the future? Because right now, their outlook is very dark and pessimistic. Their refusal to "look on the bright side" is deeply rooted. Take, for instance, the story of what the Indians call the "Trail of Tears." Just look at that name—a perfect example of glass-half-empty thinking. Yes, a few Indians apparently didn't enjoy the trip. But you know what? A lot more got a trip—a free trip, mind you—from Florida across nine states all the way to Oklahoma! Come August, I bet when the ones that are still alive hear from their relatives in Florida (okay, there aren't any left there, but assuming, for the sake of discussion, the Office of Indian Affairs had missed a few) about that legendary Florida humidity, they won't be complaining. How about the "Highway of Happiness"?

That kind of negative thinking was what resulted in the problems here at Wounded Knee Creek yesterday. President Harrison and U.S.

forces had finally established a zone of stability on the Lakota reservation in nearby Pine Ridge. But antidemocratic forces, including followers of the Ghost Dance religion, couldn't accept their loss of power. Their practice of avoiding alcohol was also designed to hurt the local economy.

And then, when the Ghost Dancers were banned, the insurgents, led by Short Bull and Kicking Bear, and 146 of their followers—men, women, and children—decided to go outside the democratic process and get themselves massacred by Colonel James Forsythe and his brave troops, who were simply trying to bring them democracy.

Americans can denounce this kind of thing from here to Tippecanoe, but when is an Indian leader—one who isn't dead, anyway—going to finally come out and denounce the Indians who keep getting themselves massacred? Not a single Indian leader—and there are still several alive—has denounced this sickness in their culture that leads to their followers constantly getting themselves massacred.

There is only one way to stop this cycle of violence: it takes a tribe. And these massacres, these stumbling blocks on the road to democracy, will only stop when Indian moderates stand up and delegitimize those who continue to force U.S. forces to massacre them.

Maybe the critics of Indian society are right—that these people just love to be killed, and we'll never be able to make them stop making us kill them. But I'm just too much of an optimist to believe that. I still believe that we can democratize the Indians, at least the ones that haven't jumped in front of our bullets or willingly let themselves become infected with smallpox.

But it's all up to them. We've given them all we can give them. And I think they can do it.

I guess I'm just a teepee-half-full kind of guy.

☆ ☆ ☆

## PART THREE: CABLE TELEVISION NEWS AND "THE WAR ON CHRISTMAS"

You may find this hard to believe, but there are times when cable news is not covering missing white women. Occasionally, they turn their attention to politics. Or, more accurately, "politics." In fact, their version of politics is to real politics what missing white women are to the crime problem in America. There's nothing that excites a Fox or CNN anchor more than a phony "controversy." Remember Ebonics? Now it's been replaced by something called "the War on Christmas," to which cable news gave more coverage last fall than they did that other war the country is currently waging. Their preferred way to "cover" an issue like this is to get two people on with opposing viewpoints, sprinkle some gunpowder on them, and watch them go at it.

But what happens if one of the people doesn't take the issue seriously? The whole thing falls down very quickly. Sam was asked to be on CNN, to debate "the War on Christmas" with a guy named Bob Knight, from the Culture and Family Institute. Here's how it went:*

**KYRA PHILLIPS (ANCHOR):** Merry Christmas or happy holidays . . . We've seen controversy, most notably prompted by the White House. It sent out cards—this card, as a matter of fact—wishing a holiday season of hope and happiness. No mention of Christmas . . . Let's start with the holiday card. What do you think, Sam?

**SEDER:** Listen, as far as the war on Christmas goes, I feel like we should be waging a war on Christmas. I mean, I believe that Christmas, it's almost proven that Christmas has nuclear weapons, can be an imminent threat to this country, that they have operative ties with terrorists, and I believe that we should sacrifice thousands of American lives in pursuit of this war on Christmas. And hundreds of billions of dollars of taxpayers' money.

---

* Edited for length and clarity.

**PHILLIPS:** Is it a war on Christmas, a war on Christians, a war on over–political correctness, or just a lot of people with way too much time on their hands?

**SEDER:** I would say probably, if I was to be serious about it, too much time on their hands, but I'd like to get back to the operational ties between Santa Claus and Al Qaeda.

**PHILLIPS:** I don't think that exists. Bob? Help me out here.

**SEDER:** We have intelligence, we have intelligence.

**PHILLIPS:** You have intel. Where exactly does your intel come from?

**SEDER:** Well, we have tortured an elf and it's actually how we got the same information from Al Libbi. It's exactly the same way the Bush administration got this info about the operational ties between Al Qaeda and Saddam. . . .

**BOB KNIGHT, CULTURE AND FAMILY INSTITUTE:** Well, first I want to compliment him on his dry humor, but this is actually a very serious subject, because a lot of people are waking up to realize that the war on Christmas is really the culmination of a war on faith and the idea that the public square has to be cleansed of any religious expression, particularly Christian religious expression.

At one time, "happy holidays" was a welcome addition to "Merry Christmas," so you wouldn't say the same thing over and over again, but a lot of people now see it as a substitute, and it's very gratuitous at times.

And it's actually insulting when you're talking about Christmas Day or a Christmas tree and you can't bring yourself to use the word for fear of offending someone. In the name of diversity, we're a less free country when that happens. . . .

**SEDER:** Yes, well, Kyra, I mean, listen, I would like Bob to tell me who is the person who has been offended by someone saying "Merry Christmas" to them? I've never met that person.

I don't celebrate Christmas. But if someone says "Merry Christmas" to me, I think, well, it's a little bit odd, it's like me saying "Happy birthday" to you on my birthday, but no one cares. . . .

What else would Bob Knight have an opportunity to do, how else would he get on television if he wasn't pretending to be attacked?

**KNIGHT:** This would be funny, except it is serious to a lot of people who have seen their faith cleansed from the public square systemically. . . .

**SEDER:** Bob, it's the holiday time, I'm not your opponent.

**KNIGHT:** Yes, you are. Yes, you are. . . .

**PHILLIPS:** People might argue that Hanukkah is just as big as Christmas.

**KNIGHT:** I have some Jewish friends and none of them say Hanukkah is as big as Christmas.

**SEDER:** Hanukkah is not a high holiday. Our high holidays are Rosh Hashanah and Yom Kippur, which I'm sure Bob has been protesting why there are not more Yom Kippur sales or Rosh Hashanah sales during those holidays. Why shouldn't there be, right, Bob?

**KNIGHT:** If that was associated with that holiday, then maybe I would join you. But it never has been.

**SEDER:** Bob, have you ever protested Martin Luther King Day not being celebrated? Do you resent when people don't say "Happy Martin Luther King Day" a month out in advance? . . .

**PHILLIPS:** Bob, I'm going to let you have the final thought.

**KNIGHT:** OK. You know, when the Nazis moved into Austria in 1936 . . .

**SEDER:** Oh, that's offensive, Bob, to raise Nazis.

**KNIGHT:** They immediately removed Christmas from the schools. You can read about it in . . . Maria von Trapp wrote the story of the von Trapp singers that's in *The Sound of Music,* and she said she sent her kids to school after the Nazis took over. And they came home and said, Mama, we can't say the word "Christmas" anymore. It's now "winter holiday."

I think that ought to disturb people . . .

**SEDER:** Kyra, that's offensive.

**KNIGHT:** . . . that we're moving toward that kind of attitude in this country.

**SEDER:** The Puritans also outlawed Christmas. The founding fathers of this country would fine you in Massachusetts if you celebrated Christmas, in the beginning. So don't talk about Nazis, Bob. I think that's really inappropriate.

Why do you have to bring hate to this Christmas and holiday season? That's so sad, Bob.

**KNIGHT:** Well, let's go to the Soviet Union then too. They had Grandfather Frost.

Well, it's the truth. You ought to read the book yourself, and maybe you'll change your mind.

**SEDER:** It's just sad that you have to raise Nazis when you're talking about Christmas and the holiday season. And we all know that

Christmas—actually, Tannenbaum, it's a German holiday. Bob, I'm really, really disappointed in you.

**KNIGHT:** I'm sorry to disappoint you, but if you can't understand the force of history . . .

**PHILLIPS:** Gentlemen, we've got to leave it there. . . .

**KNIGHT:** Well, I'd like to say "Merry Christmas," if I have the opportunity.

**SEDER:** Don't cut and run from the war on Christmas.

**PHILLIPS:** Thanks, gentlemen, talk to you later.

**KNIGHT:** Thank you.

# THE NEW YORK TIMES
## Best-Seller
# LIST OF THE FUTURE*

1 **THE BIBLE**, by God, with The Holy Spirit. (United States Government Printing Office, free; mandatory). The Word of God, quick, and powerful, and sharper than any two-edged sword, piercing even to the dividing asunder of soul and spirit, and of the joints and marrow, and a discerner of the thoughts and intents of the heart. With a new foreword by Jim Belushi.

2 **A MILLION AND ONE LITTLE PIECES**, by James Frey. (Random House, $43.95.) A memoir by the Viceroy of Iraq about his hardscrabble childhood that made him tough enough to quell the civil war in Iraq and divide it into a million and one self-governing "cantons."

3 **THE DARK LITTLE BOY AND THE iPOD**, by Thomas L. Friedman. (Farrar, Straus & Giroux, $47.95.) A columnist for The New York Times explains the connection between solving world conflict and a third-world boy owning an iPod Shuffle.

4 **THE SEA OF GALILEE DIET**, by Reverend Thomas Waterman. (Rodale, $42.95.) Also known as "The Communion Diet," a weight-loss plan built entirely around small amounts of red wine (the Blood of the Lamb) and small wafers (the Body of Christ).

5 **THE JUNGLE (UPDATED EDITION)**, by Upton Sinclair, with revisions by George A. Hormel IV. (Random House, $37.95.) Updated classic about a Chicago meatpacking plant, and how interference from the Food and Drug Administration and the Occupational Safety and Health Administration drove up consumer prices and cost Americans jobs.

6 **HARRY POTTER AND THE CROSS OF NAZARETH**, by J. K. Rowling (Scholastic, Inc., $34.95.) A young wizard realizes sorcery is evil, accepts Jesus as his personal Lord and Savior, and marries a young woman named Hermione, who wisely chose to abstain from sexual intercourse until marriage.

7 **GOD HATES YOU. WE HATE YOU**, by Laura Baker (Zondervan, $39.95.) The best-selling author of *Straight Baby on Board* explains the correct way to respond if your child says that he or she might be gay.

8 **THE METAPHOR GROWS IN THE SIMILE**, by Thomas L. Friedman (Farrar, Straus & Giroux, $42.95.) A columnist for the New York Times says that the solution to the world's economic divide is for the developed world to export metaphors to the developing world.

9 **MY TOP STORY–AND MY BOTTOM STORY**, by James D. Guckert (Random House, $39.95.) A memoir by Jeff Gannon, the 20-year veteran anchor of the CBS Evening News.

---

* In January 2007, The New York Times, responding to the scandal surrounding James Frey's fabricated memoir (and other fictionalized biographies), abandoned its separate lists for fiction and nonfiction and agreed to combine the lists under one heading.

**10** **TANGO AND 'STACHE**, by John Bolton (Scribner's, $28.95.) Vice President Bolton's guide to seducing women using nothing but natural charm, the Latin dance of love, and his "Weapon of Mustache Diplomacy."

**11** **ME STRAIGHT NOW AND REALIZE ME WAS AN ABOMINATION UNTO GOD**, by David Sedaris (Little, Brown, $31.95.) The author hilariously describes how being beaten and detained by government agents helped him to understand the error of his ways.

**12** **YOUR BODIES, GOD'S SELVES**, by Rev. Jimmy Dobson, III (Regnery, $36.95.) A guide to women's health and their dirty, obscene, disgusting reproductive systems, with suggestions on how to avoid sex, or touching yourself "down there," until marriage, and afterwards, too.

**13** **HAMMER TIME!**, by Tom DeLay (Putnam, $48.95.) A former House majority leader of the Republican Party recounts his time in prison, his conversion to Islam while in prison, and his later success on the PGA senior tour.

**14** **I THINK IT WAS THE MUSTACHE**, by Thomas L. Friedman (Farrar, Straus & Giroux, $45.95.) A columnist for the New York Times recounts his complete mental breakdown, and describes a new grooming system that he says helped him recover and become less annoying.

**15** **FARMER'S AL-MAN-ON-MAN-AC**, by Rev. Pat Robertson (Chronicle Books, $32.95.) In a newly updated edition, the secretary of the Department of Homeland Security Pat Robertson explains the connection between the extreme weather patterns and homosexuality, and how to adjust your growing season—and your property insurance coverage—accordingly.

**16** **YOU MIGHT BE A JEW IF . . . (VOL. 7)**, by Timothy Wright (Simon & Schuster, $28.95.) Another volume of the humor classic, which includes such "clues" to your being Jewish as "you're filthy," "you're a Democrat," "you stole Christmas," and "you're in Hell."

**17** **MAN ON DOG AND LOVIN' EVERY MINUTE OF IT!**, by Rick Santorum (Morrow, $42.95.) A former senator describes his long-term love affair with "Big Boy," and offers tips on love, commitment, and interspecies relationships.

**18** **WHEN THE SAINTS WENT MARCHING IN**, by Denny Hastert Jr. (Random House, $31.95.) The CEO of the "New Orleans Experience" recounts how "The Big Easy" was transformed into a family-friendly Christian theme park.

**19** **THE PURPOSE-DRIVEN LIFE**, by Jenna and Barbara Bush (Crown, $35.95.) Two daughters of a former president give advice on how to live a serious and fulfilling life with the help of tips on makeup, hangover remedies, achieving perfect ass-cleavage, and avoiding the military draft.

**20** **JUST GIVE ME ONE MORE CHANCE: I PROMISE IT WILL WORK**, by Condoleezza Rice (Little, Brown, $41.95.) The president of the United States admits that mistakes were made in the Iran War, and pleads that with just a few trillion dollars more, democracy will be possible there, or at least restoration of electricity. Foreword by Ike Turner.

# 19 · FREQUENTLY ASKED QUESTIONS ABOUT BEING A GAY REPUBLICAN CONGRESSMAN

We don't just talk about the problems in *F.U.B.A.R.*—we offer solutions. Here are a few "how-to" guides to help you navigate the new America. And lest some readers who might, shall we say, be on the other side of the political spectrum think we're excluding them, the first one is especially for them. Or, at least, one particular group of them.

*Q: Another congressman wants me to cosponsor an antigay bill. Do I sign on?*

A: Of course. It's hard to rise through the ranks as a gay-hating gay without some major gay-hating legislation under your belt. Besides, you know the guy who asked you to cosponsor? He's gay, too.

You'll be having sex with him before the thing gets out of committee. This will also make the committee hearings a lot more fun—furtive glances, yielding the balance of your time to each other, jokes about "achieving cloture," that sort of thing.

*Q: Mustaches. Your thoughts?*

A: There are three schools of thought about mustaches:

1) They make you look less gay

2) They make you look more gay

3) They make you look incredibly gay

Our feeling is the answer lies somewhere between 2 and 3. Which doesn't necessarily mean you shouldn't go for it.

Also, keep in mind that the more vocally gay-hating you are, the more gay the mustache will look. In fact, there are many things that seem ostensibly straight, but when coupled with vehement gay-hating, or any sense that you might be "trying too hard," suddenly seem incredibly gay. Like weightlifting and talking a lot about "pussy." Mustaches fall into this category.

This is known as the "Roy Cohn Paradox."

*Q: What do I say to my wife when I want to leave the house at eleven p.m. to go have sex with another man? Won't she be suspicious?*

A: This comes up a lot. And, obviously, every relationship is different. First of all, is your wife an alcoholic? From the fact that you're even asking, we're assuming the answer is no. Because if she were, you don't have to say anything. Just make her a few drinks at about nine or so, and then wait for her to pass out. The good news is that if your wife's not an alcoholic yet, she will be soon.

But until that time, you're going to need good stock excuses. Here are a few suggestions:

"Honey, that was my office calling. There's an emergency up on the

Hill. I'd really love to have sex with you now, because you're a woman and I'm a straight man, so why wouldn't I? But I have to go. Because of my country."

"Sweetheart, Carmelita forgot to clean my bathroom. So I've got to run to the park and find a clean public one. If I'm not there, I'll be at the nearest rest stop on I-87."

"I can't believe it, sweetheart. Congressman Dreier's bachelor party is tonight! I'd forgotten all about it. Can't believe that pussy hound is finally getting married. Anyway, the party is at a strip club. But don't worry—I'll look, but I won't touch. Even though I really, really love pussy. Yours, most of all. In fact, that's the reason I never touch it—because I love it too much. See ya."

"Dear, the president just called—wants me over at the White House ASAP to help him with a bill banning gay marriage. Can you believe those gays, always pushing their gay agenda? They really hate America. And God, too. They hate America and God. Don't stay up."

*Q: I'm going to be having a sexual encounter soon and I was thinking of videotaping it. Should I or shouldn't I?*

A: We realize the temptation. You're having sex, which is fun. But you're also thinking of the future you, and a period of time, perhaps—given that you're closeted—an extended period of time, in which the future you isn't going to be having sex. For times like that, you're thinking, wouldn't it be nice to be able to slip in a video or DVD of a past exploit? My masturbation reel is getting old. I'm about to have a sexual encounter. What's the harm?

Well, here's what we want you to do. Visualize the future you watching the video you're thinking of making. Nice, right? Now visualize it being played on the floor of the House of Representatives. You see, we've crunched the numbers, and the chances of any private video you make ending up becoming public is, according to current calculations, 100 percent.

So do our little exercise. If you can still get an erection and enjoy thinking of your video as it's being played on the floor of the House, then go ahead and hit that RECORD button. (And, may we say, congratulate your-self on your prodigious powers of concentration and/or sexual aggression.)

*Q: Help! Someone has found out that I'm a gay-hating gay and they're trying to blackmail me. What do I do?*

A: Blackmailers are no different than terrorists. And as we've learned time and time again, negotiating with these people is flat-out wrong. It only encourages more of them and makes it harder for the next victim.

*Q: So you're saying I should stand firm?*

A: What are you, crazy? Of course not. You should give in. I mean, we understand you. But after all the gay-hating you've done, the liberal media is not going to be as fair-minded about things. So, yes, if you can, try to drive down the price, stall them, tell them you're waiting for a check, whatever you think you can do, but definitely give in.

*Q: But what if I just don't have the money?*

A: You mean because you've been spending all your money on your secret web of gay lovers?

*Q: Yes.*

A: That's cute.

*Q: Well?*

A: There is actually a solution. You're a congressman, right? That means you have access to sensitive information. And information is money, if you just get it to the right people.

*Q: You're saying I should sell state secrets?*

A: Hey, it's not easy being a closeted gay-hating gay. Do you want to stay in the closet or don't you? Besides, it's the non-gay-haters who are the real enemy of the United States.

*Q: What do I do if I get caught with another man?*

A: It depends on whether you're caught by a staffer or your wife. If it's a staffer, this may not be what you want to hear, but you're the boss, and, as such, you have a responsibility. Therefore, there's really only one thing you can do: you have to fire them. Make up a reason—embezzling and sexual harassment are both good—and fire them. And you have to do it immediately. That way, if they go public, you can say their charges were simply to deflect attention away from their own behavior. But let them know that if they do go public, you'll destroy them. Call Tom DeLay's office for help.

If it's your wife that catches you, you're going to have to be honest with her. Sit her down, be very gentle and loving. Take her hand, look her in the eye, and calmly say, "Honey, how much money is this going to cost me? I'll give you as much as you want. But no divorce until after the election."

In the event the above advice fails, and you find yourself about to be outed . . .

\* \* \*

## THE RNC GUIDE TO BEING OUTED AS A GAY-HATING GAY

Living a life as a closeted gay-hating gay isn't easy. But if you're a Republican officeholder, it's even harder. To even have won the Republican primary, you must have had to do some serious gay-hating.

That's all good—that just means you're a very good gay-hating gay. The downside is that when you're actually voting on and even sponsoring gay-hating legislation, you draw the attention of non-gay-hating gays. These types can be very mean. Apparently, their lack of self-loathing has clouded their thinking, rendering them unable to see the beautiful logic of what you're trying to do. Their misguided solution to this is to try to "out" you.

When they do this, they will often point out your gay activities along-side your antigay activities. Unfortunately, the result is often that the public is also unable to see the logic of your gay-hating gay lifestyle.

This can often leave you feeling lonely and isolated, as well as put a severe dent in your gay sex life. Well, unlike your former friends, the Republican Party is not going to let you down.

Note: the following suggestions are meant to be employed sequentially. Try each stage we suggest. If one of them works, great—you're free to go back to your gay-hating gay lifestyle. Just ease back in, and use discretion. If trouble persists, however, move on to the next level.

### STAGE ONE: RUBBER/GLUE

First, never admit anything. Unless you have to. Or unless you've been stupid enough to make videotapes (see "Frequently Asked Questions About Being a Gay Republican Congressman"). To liberally borrow an old phrase, the best defense is a good offense. There're always going to be rumors out there. You should ignore them as long as you can, but when some liberal elite gay group uses them to attack you, turn it right back at 'em. When they accuse you of being gay, respond with "Oh, yeah? I'm not gay. You're gay. You're the gay one!"

Obviously, if the group that attacked you is an avowedly gay group, calling them gay might not be the most effective tactic. Instead, you should issue a statement saying that you "deplore personal smears" and "the politics of personal destruction." And always refer to the groups attacking you as "homosexuals" trying to advance "the homosexual lifestyle."

### STAGE TWO: HOW CAN I BE GAY—I'VE GOT A WIFE AND KIDS!

Okay, so you're in a real battle here. Usually the first two stages are enough for the mainstream press. But perhaps you've got some blogger or an actual, nonhack reporter fueling this situation. You're going to have to call in some reinforcements.

Arrange to be seen in public with your wife and children. There should be lots of smiles and (appropriate) touching. Never go anywhere without them. This may sound unpleasant for you, but when you're in the presence of a photographer or reporter, try kissing your wife. This is important, however: it has to be a real kiss. It should not look like a kiss by a man who's really gay but pretending to like kissing a woman, even though you're really gay and pretending to like kissing a woman. From our feedback, we've been told it helps to visualize a current or ex-boyfriend while kissing your wife.

If you don't have children, get some. Nieces and nephews are good. Even kids from the neighborhood. Or those "Fresh Air Fund" kids, where they take kids from the inner city and let them spend the summer in the suburbs. The kids get fresh air, and you get some time to try to salvage your political career and your marriage. That's called a win-win situation.

## STAGE THREE: COUNTERATTACK

So clearly the kid thing didn't work. Hopefully, though, you made some new friends, and maybe got some free yard-work out of the whole deal. Obviously, the non-gay-hating gay bastards are really serious about you. It's time for the major counterattack.

If you've got some dirt on the groups attacking you, use it. If not, you're going to have to resort to the PR technique called MSU ("Making Shit Up"). If you feel like your statements at this stage don't completely make sense, that's okay; they're not supposed to. But let's face it, you're desperate.

You're free to make up your own (that's the essence, and the fun, of MSU), but since we realize that having your career and life and marriage and gay sex life completely unravel can be distracting, here are some suggestions:

★ My opponents have proven again and again how much they hate America

★ My opponents have proven again and again how much they hate God

★ My opponents have proven again and again how much they hate families

★ My opponents have proven again and again how much they hate [any good thing]

★ This is just another attempt by my opponents to try to get God out of schools

★ My opponents hate me because I support the troops

★ My opponents are simply trying to distract attention away from their own problems

## STAGE FOUR: RETREAT

We're not gonna bullshit you here. You're in trouble. If you're still here, it's time to consider giving some ground. This doesn't mean you have to admit anything, however. It just means you need to ratchet down the situation. Get out of the public eye, let things calm down a little. If you're willing to exploit your family a bit (and, hey, obviously you are—you're in a fake marriage for political reasons and your wife probably doesn't know it yet), they can be useful in gaining some sympathy for you.

Before you leave the public eye, you should issue a statement, something like:

"Because of the unwarranted and personal attacks on me by homosexual smear groups, I would like to ask the press to grant me and my family some personal space at this difficult time. I would also like to say how much we appreciate the incredible outpouring of encouragement shown by my many supporters."

## STAGE FIVE: RESIGNATION

Well, you've come to the end of the road. You're resigning. Obviously, you'd made video or audiotapes, and your opponents got hold of one of them. That wasn't smart, but it's in the past now, and we hope you've at least got a copy, so you can enjoy it at a later date.

Unless the video and/or audiotapes have been played, with any luck, there's still a chance that giving up your office will allow you to hang on to some semblance of your gay-hating gay life. The main difference will be that you won't be able to actually sponsor and introduce gay-hating legislation. But there are plenty of lobbying groups and "family" organizations that could use your expertise.

At this stage, everyone has their own way of handling things, but here are some tips for the resignation process:

* Why are you resigning? To spend more time with your wife and children, of course. Unfortunately, even though this isn't really why you're resigning, it probably will be one of the sad consequences.

* For the actual resignation press conference, you're going to need your wife. Given where you are in the process, there's a pretty good chance she's going to need to be pretty drunk, or heavily medicated, to get through this. That's fine. But you don't want her too drunk. This can look bad. Pay special attention to her lipstick: you don't want any smeared on her teeth. Trust us. Reads as drunk, even if she's stone-cold sober.

* Be optimistic. Talk about how much you're looking forward to the future and new opportunities. And, in fact, there are new opportunities. Now that you'll be out of the public light, the gay part of being a gay-hating gay is going to be a lot easier.

# 20 · HOW TO SPEAK RELIGIOUSLY

Fortunately, until the Apocalypse arrives, Bush has pledged to have the utmost respect and tolerance for all religions and treat everyone equally, regardless of how "Christian" they are.

Really?

Of course not. Don't be ridiculous. But we almost had you there, didn't we? This is a guy, after all, who, in the run-up to the 2000 presidential campaign, said: "I feel like God wants me to run for president. I can't explain it, but I sense my country is going to need me. Something is going to happen . . ."*

And do you know what that something was? ABC's *According to Jim*.

Actually, we don't know what he was referring to (but *According to Jim* did premiere the very same year Bush took office—draw your own conclusions), but the point is, for the time being, Jesus is Number One. As

---

* *The Faith of George W. Bush*, Stephen Mansfield (Tarcher, 2003).

General William G. "Jerry" Boykin, Bush's deputy undersecretary of defense for intelligence, put it while talking about a battle against a Muslim Somali warlord, "I knew my God was bigger than his. I knew that my God was a real God and his was an idol."

Yeah, sure, it's all talk now, but the guy's got guns, and says stuff like "We in the army of God, in the house of God, kingdom of God have been raised for such a time as this."

A time like what? A time to kick your nonbelieving apostate ass, that's what.

So what are your options? As we see it, you've got two choices. You can:

1) Convert. But the obvious problem here is that, from the fact that you're even reading this, we take it you're probably not capable of true conversion. Not to mention the fact that we hear there are pretty high fees and uniforms required.

2) Pass. Easy enough, right? Wrong. These people can sense insincerity. It's not enough to walk around yelling "Jesus is Number One, man!" or "Dude, I am so into God right now!" It's more subtle than that, and it's harder than it looks. So, to help out, we present:

\* \* \*

## THE F.U.B.A.R. GUIDE TO SPEAKING RELIGIOUSLY

*"Christian"*
Synonymous with "American." To be used interchangeably, i.e.:

"I'm rooting for the Christians in this game."

"We were uncomfortable in Paris, then we ran into some Christians."

"Are you Canadian?"—"No, Christian."

"I buy only Christian products."

*"American"*
Synonymous with "human."

*"Our Muslim brothers and sisters"*
Not human.

*"Bless your heart"*
All-purpose phrase that can mean many things, most of them bad. Especially handy when speaking to or about a nonbeliever. When the nonbeliever identifies him- or herself as a nonbeliever, you say, "Bless your heart." Which means, "Bless your heart, because you are going to Hell."

*"I'll pray for you."*
"You are going to Hell."

*"Hate the sin, not the sinner"*
This is what you say about a non-Christian person you disapprove of. Or any Christian, really. It's most often said about homosexuals. It's nice, because it lets you get out your hate but still sound Christian. What it means is: "I hate the sin, and the sinner." Unless, of course, the person saying it is a homosexual. In which case, it means: "I hate myself."

*"Enemies of the United States"*
This is used to describe non-Christians in other countries. Also used to describe non-Christians in this country.

*"Jesus Christ"*
The Son of God. Not to be used as an exclamation. Unless you're exclaiming about the Son of God. For instance, "Jesus Christ! . . . is whom I love."

*"The Word of God"*
Refers to the Bible. But not the entire Bible. Is usually used in denouncing something, most often homosexuals. Parts of the Bible not included when generally referring to the Bible or the "Word of God" are:

"If there is a poor man among you, one of your brothers, in any of the towns of the land which the LORD your God is giving you, you shall not harden your heart, nor close your hand to your poor brother; but you shall freely open your hand to him, and generously lend him sufficient for his need in whatever he lacks." (Deuteronomy 15:7)

"Sell all that you have, and give to the poor." (Mark 10:21)

"My brothers, what use is it for a man to say he has faith when he does nothing to show it? Can that faith save him? Suppose a brother or a sister is in rags with not enough food for the day, and one of you says, 'Good luck to you, keep yourselves warm, and have plenty to eat,' but does nothing to supply their bodily needs, what is the good of that? So with faith; if it does not lead to action, it is in itself a lifeless thing." (James 2:14–17)

"Sell your possessions and give to charity." (Luke 12:33)

"It is easier for a camel to pass through the eye of a needle than for a rich man to enter the kingdom of God." (Matthew 19:24)

"When you pray, you shall not be as the hypocrites, for they love to stand and pray in the synagogues and in the corners of the streets, that they may be seen by men." (Matthew 6:5)

### "Blessed"
As in, "I've been blessed," or "the Lord has blessed me." This means: "I have a lot of money and have chosen to ignore the verses quoted above, but at least I'm giving props to my financial adviser, Jesus, who, by the way, was Jewish."

### "Lifestyle"
Homosexuals. Yes, there is a straight "lifestyle," too, but the word is used only to designate the homosexual lifestyle.

## *"Family values"*

As in, "I believe in family values." This can mean a variety of things. For example:

"I don't like to pay taxes for government services."

"I'm afraid of homosexuals."

"I'm afraid of black people."

"I'm afraid of foreigners."

"I believe Rush just had a bad-back problem."

"I think the fifties was the best time in U.S. history."

"I'm white."

## *"God bless America"*

"My political speech is over."

## *"Us" and "We"*

White, Christian Americans. For example:

"We need to stop illegal immigrants from overrunning our country."

"The internment of Japanese during World War II was wrong, but our country was under attack."

## *"Evolution"*

Absurd theory that holds that the earth is over four thousand years old.

## ETIQUETTE GUIDE FOR THE NEW AMERICA

★ When ordering a drink: "I'll have a martini, the way Jesus would have liked it: very dry."

★ When reaching orgasm: "Oh, I'm about to come all ye faithful!"

★ When gassing up your car: "Fill 'er up . . . with the power of God unto salvation to every one that believeth." (What many call "super.")

★ When paying a large dinner tab: "Only the eternal sacrifice of Jesus on the cross could pay this bill!"

★ When you walk into a room and it smells bad: "It smells like something died then rose again in here!"

★ When a woman with a pleasing-looking behind walks by: [loudly] "Can I get some forgiveness with that shake!"

# 21 · HOW TO WIN FRIENDS AND CONVERT REPUBLICANS (Or Just Convert Republicans)

Obviously, in a perfect world, there would be no Republicans, just like there would be no cancer or poisonous scorpions. But we don't live in a perfect world. Unfortunately, until we really get a chance to work with stem cells, we're gonna have to live with cancer and Republicans. That doesn't mean there's nothing that can be done.

You can try to plant a seed of truth in their mind, one that will grow and start cracking the foundation of illogic, fear, and resentment that their Republicanism is built on.

Don't expect too much. Undoubtedly, there are statistics and studies on seed-to-plant yield ratios, but we're also pretty sure we couldn't understand them. Just know that by planting a seed here and there, we will all be one step closer to a Republican-free world.* A freedom forest, if you will.

---

\* Of course, like smallpox, we will want to keep at least one Republican in a lab somewhere, maybe in Switzerland—just in case they make a comeback and we need to develop a vaccine.

The key to our strategy is based on the simple reality that for Republicans, all politics is identity politics. You can't convince a Republican that gravity exists unless they think that you're like them, that you're one of them. To paraphrase the bible of conversion—literally, the Bible: Unto the Republicans, you must become as a Republican.*

Now, Republicans don't wear signs saying "I'm a Republican." At least, not all of them. Nor do they all drive Hummers. And there are many different types. To help you in your task, we've taken the liberty of identifying the primary Republican archetypes. This field guide doesn't describe every kind of Republican—new species are being discovered every day—but the most common varieties are here.

We also give you ways to get in there with them. Each one of them has a weak point—a detail in their lives that, unbeknown to them, is actually incompatible with their Republicanism. After you find it, you form common ground around it, and work from there.

☆　☆　☆

## THE MIDWESTERN MIDDLE-MANAGEMENT GUY

*Who?*

★ He's your girlfriend's stepfather.

★ He lives in Michigan or Minnesota. He works nine to five, drives a pickup or a Jeep or an SUV or something else with four big wheels, which growls when you gun it.

★ He served in the army or the marines, he doesn't like elitist college types, and he definitely doesn't like hippies—though he did go to college and probably did some drugs.

---

* I Corinthians 9:20: "And unto the Jews I became as a Jew, that I might gain the Jews; to them that are under the law, as under the law, that I might gain them that are under the law . . . I am made all things to all [men], that I might by all means save some."

★ Let's call him "Jim."

★ He's a real potential get.

*Where?*

★ Out to dinner at Applebee's. Or Bennigan's. Or T.G.I.Whatever the Fuck's. Suffice it to say it's poorly lit, the margaritas are mostly crushed ice and cherry syrup, and there's a bunch of crap on the walls.

★ They also serve an oriental chicken salad, which is "oriental" because it has canned mandarin oranges in it.

★ Jim *loves* this restaurant. He and his friends come here after work, and, sometimes, on a Friday, he takes the whole family.

*How?*

Speak his language . . . gain his trust. Now it's time to convert him, and everything you do from this moment on becomes crucial (no pressure).

★ Time to order. Do you get:

A) The oriental chicken salad (with mandarin oranges!)

B) The mozzarella sticks

C) Prime rib with steak fries

D) The veggie burger

The answer is simple: you get (B) the mozzarella sticks and (C) prime rib. Don't eat like a girl in front of this guy or he's not gonna respect you—remember, you're a man's man; for the time being, you've never heard of *Queer Eye for the Straight Guy* and you lettered in something.

Now get a drink, but order a drink with only one ingredient—and not wine, Nancy! Order by asking only for "a beer." Should be domestic. Nothing imported. But don't say "domestic"—say "American." A glass? "Are you serious?" Don't wait for the waitress to answer, just say "no."

★ Time to engage him in conversation. You turn to Jim and say:

A) "I read a great piece in the *New York Times Book Review* on the plane flight about the new Philip Roth."

B) "Did you see *Desperate Housewives* last night? Friggin' hysterical."

C) "Boy, the waitress has a hot rack."

D) "I really felt like the 'independent commission' on the Dan Rather/*60 Minutes 2*/Bush service-record scandal dropped the ball."

The answer: (C). Forge a relationship based on the objectification of the waitress. Say it in front of your girlfriend and get extra points!* Extra bonus points for an "Am I right?" and adding a high five.

★ Next, you look around the Applebee's and say: "What a pleasure!" Because:

A) "I find eating in crappy restaurants with pitchforks and wagon wheels and other random shit on the walls weirdly pleasurable."

B) "I really enjoy spending quality time with family."

C) "The offerings on the menu seem generic to me, and often I worry that big-box chain-store eateries are negatively impacting the economic model for mom-and-pop shops and homogenizing our culture, wouldn't you agree?"

D) "There's too many hippies in most restaurants these days, but not this one—it's weird!"

The correct answer is either (B) or (D). Your sudden burst of conservatism should surprise and perhaps confuse your girlfriend's stepfather. Chances are, he's going to say "I hear that" about the hippies, and then give you a look of confusion—but a satisfied confusion.

---

* You might want to make sure she's on board with this whole conversion thing first.

Now that you've succeeded in establishing your bona fides, whatever you do, don't use the phrase "bona fides." Order another beer. Order Jim a beer. We're rockin'.

Now Jim is starting to think, Boy, this guy may be even more conservative than *I* am—it's time to . . .

### Move in for the Kill

Jim is a guy who works hard and thinks other people should work hard. He thinks he's been screwed over by society.

He's right.

You have to appeal to his feeling that his hard work hasn't paid off for him.

He's right.

Jim blames "liberal professors" and the "elite."

You need to show him that the people getting one over on him aren't the liberal hippies and coffee-drinking elite—it's the Republican politicians who are the real elite screwing him over.

So the next beer you order, start to complain about beer prices back in your hometown.

Say something to the effect of "Wow, it's a real pleasure paying two dollars for a beer—I don't have any of that Dick Cheney money to throw around."

Say it like it's an expression. Put a real emphasis in your voice, like "Dick Cheney money" is the same kind of phrase as "jazz hands" or "busy as a beaver."*

Your prey bites: "What do you mean, Dick Cheney money?"

You say: "You know what I mean by Dick Cheney/Halliburton money, don't you?"

If he's still not biting, order more beer and try again.

Bring out the big guns: continue on your Cheney riff in your best sarcastic voice:† "Man, I would love to be in a position to give a company

---

* Do not say "jazz hands."
† That's "sarcastic," not "kitschy," and definitely NOT "campy."

billions of dollars in no-bid contracts, like, say, $11.7 billion in no-bid contracts, and then still be getting anywhere from $150,000 to $200,000 a year added to my vice president's salary.

"Hey, I like Dick Cheney as much as the next guy—I mean for a guy who went to Yale—but why is he getting paid by this company he's giving money back to? Back at the garage, we call that a kickback.*

"How much do you make again, Jim? Huh . . .

"I wish I were like Dick Cheney and I could own 400,000 stock options in the company that was nearing bankruptcy before I came to office because of asbestos . . ."

On to:

"As much as Dick Cheney pisses me off, I wouldn't mind bein' his kid—I mean not the lesbian one—'cuz now that there's no estate tax for millionaires, his kids are going to get buckets of tax-free money. 'Course my taxes will probably go up so that he doesn't have to pay his millionaire's tax. Oh, well, these mozzarella sticks are the best."

Closing comment:

"Ah, what are you going to do . . . I guess next time I may vote the Democrats. Politicians are all scumbags, but at least those guys don't screw me in front of my face. Should we get some cheese wings?"

And your work is done!

Ready to try for the next level of difficulty? Let's move on to . . .

☆ ☆ ☆

## THE PLUTOCRAT

*Who?*
★ He's your boss, or your boss's boss, or the guy who manages your boss's boss's hedge fund.

---

* Don't be specific about which garage—it's just a good way of getting to "kickback."

★ He's dedicated his adult life (and some good portion of his adolescence) to accruing and managing huge piles of money. He has been very successful at this. There's also a strong chance his folks gave him a ton of money and, despite the fact that he believes people should pull themselves up by their bootstraps, he's very much in favor of getting rid of what he calls the "death tax."

★ He lives in Greenwich, Connecticut, although he has a pied-à-terre on the Upper East Side. He thinks the city is full of animals (read: blacks, Latinos, Pakistanis). His ex-wife lives in Cape May, his current money lives in the Caymans.

★ He plays golf on the weekends, sends his kids to exclusive private schools. He has one black friend.

★ He's an Ivy Leaguer.

★ He hasn't spent less than $300 on a bottle of wine in fifteen years.

★ He owns a lot of companies, the kind that exist to buy and sell other companies.

★ Let's call him Lawrence.

### Where?

★ Playing eighteen holes at Lawrence's club, aka "The Club."

★ Lawrence is an avid golfer. You'll have to at least be able to pretend to know what you're doing if you're going to convert Lawrence, so you better start practicing now.

★ It's a beautiful spring day—rolling hills, green grass, minorities cutting the lawn and hauling big bags of clubs around. Let's get to work!

*How?*

Gain his trust. Speak his language and dress his dress . . .

★ Find what you would think is a parody of an asshole's golf outfit. Wear that.

★ Speak in clipped tones and perfect grammar, making sure to indicate with everything you say and do that you're sort of vaguely irritated that other people are alive.

★ Talk only about things that cost more than they're worth and have whole magazines dedicated to them—cigars, fancy sports cars, architecture, mutual funds, wine, boats.

★ Lament the lack of quality haberdasheries in Westchester.

★ Allude to the fact of having, but don't actually admit to having, a mistress.

Time for the icebreaker. For your opening line, do you:

A) Admit to waking up at eleven and expose your lack of concern at having a "productive day."

B) Remark that you "feel uncomfortable with the lack of diversity at this country club."

C) Ask, "What's a hedge fund?"

D) Say, "This is just what I needed—a client of mine took me to the [insert professional sports team here] game. The seats were general admission, and I haven't been able to get the stink off me for days."

The answer is (D). Feel free to substitute "my girlfriend's parents were in town from the Midwest—they're teachers [insert knowing eye roll]" for the sporting event, so it sounds like "my girlfriend's parents were in town from the Midwest—they're teachers—and I haven't been able to get the stink off me for days."

The game begins. You purposely, or not so purposely, hook the ball to the right and it lands in the woods.

Rather offhandedly, do you say:

A) "Man, that one got away from me—just like the Republican Party."

B) "My game is off . . . I saw a documentary about Darfur last night and I guess I can't focus."

C) "That ball is as lost as fiscal responsibility under a Republican regime."

D) "If we had a national single-payer health-care program I could finally get someone to look at my nagging elbow injury."

The answer is (A). Though (C) will also work.

When Lawrence looks up from his tee and says "Wha? . . . " you turn on the juice—focus on the way that the Republican Party has strayed from its original tenets. Like . . .

★ Self-sufficiency.

★ Fiscal responsibility.

★ Hard work.

★ Strict adherence to the Constitution.

And then add:

★ "Sure seems a shame that the party of Lincoln has become the party of Jerry Falwell."

★ "Bill Frist is on his knees sucking up to these radical Christianist lunatics—did you see him at that *Justice Sunday*? If things keep going this way, we may have to do some praying *off* the golf course!"

★ "Even old-school Republicans like John Danforth are freaked out about this.* Maybe we oughta be freaked out, too, huh?"

★ "How do you think Mrs. Lawrence (hot trophy wife) is going to feel about wearing a burka?"

★ "How long are we going to tolerate these bad-suited loonies?"

★ "With 'Bush One' a guy could do business—looks like the apple rolled pretty far from the tree and ended up in the Jesus bunker." (You might want to add a "know-what-I-mean?")

You've done your job—you've planted the seeds of Lawrence's discontent. To nail it down, add:

"What do you say we bag the golf and hit a strip club?"

☆ ☆ ☆

## THE SUPERJEWISH GRANDMA

*Who?*

★ Your grandma.

★ Or, if you're not Jewish, your Jewish friend's grandma.

★ Or anyone like semi-employable actor Ron Silver.

---

* "In the Name of Politics," John C. Danforth, *New York Times,* March 30, 2005: "By a series of recent initiatives, Republicans have transformed our party into the political arm of conservative Christians. The elements of this transformation have included advocacy of a constitutional amendment to ban gay marriage, opposition to stem cell research involving both frozen embryos and human cells in petri dishes, and the extraordinary effort to keep Terri Schiavo hooked up to a feeding tube.

"Standing alone, each of these initiatives has its advocates, within the Republican Party and beyond. But the distinct elements do not stand alone. Rather they are parts of a larger package, an agenda of positions common to conservative Christians and the dominant wing of the Republican Party."

* She's religious but not THAT religious. She's probably Reform or Conservative. Her Judaism is largely a matter of knowing how to cook brisket, knowing which celebrities are and are not Jewish, and refusing to buy a Volkswagen.

* And, crucially, her Republicanism depends almost 100 percent on her belief that Republicans are "STRONGER ON ISRAEL."

* Let's call her Grandma Ron Silver.

*Where?*

* The buffet at her retirement complex in Delray Beach, Florida.

* The food stinks, but keep your head in the game—if every Jew who voted for George W. Bush in 2004 had gone the other way, we wouldn't be losing American soldiers in Iraq right now.

*How?*

Speak her language . . .

Getting on Grandma Ron's good side shouldn't be too tough—she is your grandmother, after all. But we need her to be extra-favorably inclined toward you, so you:

* Drop a few Yiddish phrases into the conversation. Don't know any? Just make some up. She'll assume she's just forgotten.

* Make sure you shave.

* Tell her you've been studying for the MCATs, the GMATs, and the LSATs.

* In the event that you are actually talking to Ron Silver, gush about *Time Cop*—"You totally stole that movie from Van Damme, and you were so good, you made him even better."

Grandma Ron's line of questioning is going to be relatively predictable. When she says, "So, are you seeing anyone?" do you reply:

A) "Oh, who can think about love with all that's going on in the world?"

B) "Yes, a black girl."

C) "Yes, an Asian girl."

D) "Yes, a Latina girl."

E) "Nah, I think my standards are too high—I'm looking for a combination of you and Ariel Sharon."

The correct answer is (E). It allows you to force the subject to Israel. When Grandma Ron responds, "Things are so bad over there," do you say:

A) "Yeah, that's what you get when a nation is taken hostage by fundamentalists who are 'so Jewish' that they think the Torah tells them to hate Arabs."

B) "Tell me about it—I guess our four billion dollars in annual aid is not enough to get them to stop building illegal settlements on other people's property."

C) "What's the difference between apartheid and not letting millions of Palestinians have citizenship or their own country again?"

D) "I gotta say that a lot of those George Bush types sure seem to support Israel, though!"

The correct answer is (D). You'll know you've led Grandma Ron down the perfect road when she says: "Yes, they do."

Now move in for the kill. Casually note something like: "Yeah . . . sure is nice that those Republicans controlling Congress are such fervent backers of Israel. It's just a shame that the reason folks like Tom DeLay are such big backers of the Jewish state is that they believe all Jews have to move back there before the End Times can arrive, so they can all die in a terrible rapture and only Tom DeLay and his friends will be left. But I guess we'll cross that bridge when it collapses into the Lake of Fire . . . "

It might be hard, but you have to press on!

"This is great tuna fish, Grandma Ron. I love how they mix in the pickles. Oh, say, if the Republicans have their way and Israel is surrounded by its enemies and ultimately destroyed, do you know how to get to be one of the ones who gets to sit at the throne of God, instead of one of the ones who descend into the fiery pit, as prophesied and fervently awaited by Bill Frist?"

Or, "I sure am glad I reserved my space on the right-hand side of God, because as I'm sure you know only one-third of Jews are going to be able to sit there while the other two-thirds are smote and cast into eternal damnation. At least that's the way folks like Tom DeLay see it goin' down. But one-third is pretty cool. Besides, we'll have all of biblical Judea and Samaria for a couple of years. And, at least, the ones who drive us into the sea won't be Arabs! You reserved your seat, right, Grandma? At the side of the throne? Grandma?"

Grandma Ron is now feeling faint, and it's not the pickles. It's a perfect time to . . . mention how evangelical Christianity has taken such strong hold in American institutions that Jewish air force cadets are being harassed.*

When you revive her, she'll be yours.

* * *

## BORN-AGAIN GIRL

*Who?*
She's a twenty-five-year-old blond former homecoming queen and born-again Christian from some state that starts with A and has stickers about evolution on its science textbooks.

---

* "Air Force Cadets See Religious Harassment," Robert Weller, ABC News, April 19, 2005.

*Where?*

Perhaps talking too loudly about Jesus on a Greyhound bus. Or handing out pamphlets in Times Square.

*How?*

Speak her language. In this case, you want to determine *her* born-again bona fides.*

When you meet her, say, "I'm just on the way to get my abstinence pledge reframed." If she can recommend the place where she got hers framed, you're in luck.†

Say "Praise Jesus" whenever possible. "How are you today?" "I'm fine, praise Jesus." "Where are you from originally?" "Cleveland, praise Jesus." Et cetera. You can sometimes just say "Praise Him." She'll know who you're talking about.

Move in for the kill. It's easy. You just get her drunk and take her virginity. And in the morning, point out that she's not going to Heaven anymore . . . so she might as well be a Democrat.

---

* Again, "bona fides" . . . no.

† You may be in more luck than you know—one Texas study reveals that women with abstinence pledges are up to six times more likely to engage in oral sex. (Note: Yes, we *are* writing this from a male perspective. Why? First, we're male. Second, nine times out of ten, changing a Republican's mind is highly difficult for women, because that's simply not their place in society. Or, at least, in Republican society.)

# 22 · GOING UNDERGROUND

If you made it this far and none of this has worked, you've got one option left. You tried the fight; now it's time for the flight. In fact, studies have shown that the Bush administration actually provokes a fight-*and*-flight reaction.

And even if you feel like you're doing fine, that you just want a chance to put all this into practice, that's okay, too. Just keep this chapter handy. They're not always going to give a lot of warning, you know.

And if you're ready to go now, put down the passport and the fake mustache. Yes, you're going underground, but this isn't your traditional kind of underground. Here's what we mean.

☆ ☆ ☆

## GOING UNDERGROUND—THE F.U.B.A.R. FAQ

*Q. Underground—isn't that a bit sixties-ish?*

A: Ha-ha. Keep up that attitude—and see how well it plays down in Guantánamo. Maybe it is a bit "sixties-ish," but so was Cointelpro. That was the name of the counterintelligence program the FBI used to spy on *anyone*—but especially those the FBI (or, mostly, J. Edgar Hoover) deemed to be "dissidents" (pretty much anybody). The program ran from 1956 till 1971. Go Google it. But do yourself a favor, do it at the Internet café around the corner, because the Patriot Act is a souped-up Cointelpro for the oughts. As the godfather of the Patriot Act, J. Edgar himself, said: "The forces which are most anxious to weaken our internal security are not always easy to identify." In other words, the less likely subversive a person seems to be, the more likely he or she or you is to be subversive. So you don't want to seem subversive, but you don't want to seem unsubversive.

*Q: What? But why?*

A: Why what? Why are they coming for you? We don't know and you don't know—and they don't need to tell you. Under Sections 215 and 505 of the Patriot Act, which the White House is now urging Congress to make permanent, federal agents can comb through your medical records, the books you've borrowed from the library, videos you've rented, church-attendance records, travel records, financial data of any kind, and Web sites you've visited. And not just without your consent but without your knowledge.

*Q: Don't they have to get permission? Don't they need to show probable cause?*

A: You might also recall a few news items about Bush claiming the authority to authorize the NSA to monitor phone calls *within* the United States with no court order.

*Q: Yikes.*

A: A reasonable response. The question is: What are you going to do about it? Start your planning when they are busting through the door? Did you forget how Ashcroft wanted to have cable guys and postal workers spy on anybody in their homes and file a report if they saw a poster of Che Guevara? Or maybe you never heard the stories of the two teachers from Cedar Rapids who were arrested in September of 2004 for simply being in the vicinity of a Bush/Cheney campaign event and talking about their disagreement with Bush's policies?

*Q: Who's doing all this investigating?*

A: Given that they don't need to tell you you're even being investigated, you're not likely to learn who "they" are. "They" could be anyone. But [un]rest assured, they will come. The FBI is coming for you; or maybe the INS; maybe even the ATF or the NSA. Or the ITS. Who's the ITS? We have no idea. That's the point.

*Q: How will they find me?*

A: It's actually quite easy. In fact, they probably already have. They could start with Google or any other search engine on the Web. Want to have some fun? Search for "reverse phone-number lookup." Enter your home phone-number in one of the sites that come up. In the unlikely event you're not staring at your information right now, have you ever filled out a form? Yeah? Ever included your address and/or Social Security number and/or taxpayer ID number and/or cell or home or work phone? Ever bought anything at a supermarket?* Ever gone to a doctor?† Opened a bank account?

---

* RFID chips.
† http://www.theleftcoaster.com/archives/001181.php.

What about the Internet? Amazon is great, but *please* tell me you're not putting your credit card number on the Internet and then sitting there asking us, How will they find me?

They'll find you, chief. It's only a matter of time.

*Q: Okay, okay. They can find me. So what am I supposed to do about it now?*

A: Great question. Let's get to work. The key to our strategy is decreasing what's called your signal-to-noise ratio. One way to do this is by decreasing your signal. That's the way most people would do it. How'd it work for them? Next time you're in Guantánamo, you can ask them. They'll be the ones in the orange jumpsuits.

The better way is to increase your noise.

*Q: You lost me.*

A: Plainly put, decreasing your signal-to-noise ratio by increasing your noise-to-signal ratio means that instead of following your natural instinct to put out as *little* information on yourself as possible, you do the opposite: you increase the amount of information until they have no idea where or what the real you might be.

Look, there is no longer any point in trying to hide from them; they have your Social Security number. They have your address. They have a list of every item you've ever purchased. They have everything. Soon there will be a national ID card, fingerprints. You know they're experimenting with GPS bracelets for foreign visitors (not criminals—just visitors). It's over, dawg.

*Q: So there's nothing I can do?*

A: Actually, there is one thing. You have to use the system against itself. The only answer is to send so much information on yourself out into the world that no one could possibly figure out how much of it is real—the idea is to become like a submarine sending out all those little heat pods to throw off the incoming torpedoes.

Get it?

*Q: No. No, I don't.*

A: That's fine. We'll go slow, we're actually getting paid by the page.

*Q: Seriously?*

A: Actually, yes. It's a dirty little secret about the book business.

*Q: I'm surprised.*

A: We were, too. You were probably wondering why that "how to be a gay Republican" chapter was so big—now you know. If we knew how to type faster, we'd be making a lot more money.

*Q: Now that you mention it, I was . . . Hey you're dragging this out on purpose—in fact, this very question is a filler! WTF!*

A: Bingo. All right, let's move on. (Interestingly, "move on" comes from the phrase "get a move on," which is an American English colloquialism dating back to 1888. A "movable feast," on the other hand, is an ecclesiastical feast that does not occur on a fixed date each year. For example, Easter).

*Q: Jesus, can we get back to going underground?*

A: Sorry. (Sam just bought a house—mortgage payments don't grow on trees, you know.) Okay, here are some techniques:

*Junk Mail: The Conductor of Your Underground Railroad.*
You know all that junk mail you get? All those requests to sign up for credit cards, refinancing, free magazine subscriptions, army recruitment forms? All the stuff you reflexively throw in the trash without reading? Think of all those worthless pieces of paper as your ticket stubs to freedom.

Stop throwing them away, and start sending them back. We want you to start filling in every single form, no matter how irritating, and then return them—you want to subscribe to every magazine, you want to join every political organization, you want to sign up for every promotional offer and enter every sweepstakes.

But here's the catch: Each time you send in the card, you alter your name, and your address, ever so slightly. Let's say, for example, that your name is Sam Seder and that you live at 3 Maple Drive, Apt. #10, New York, NY 10021.

When you get a promotion offering you three months of a free subscription to *Woman's Journal*, you send back the card . . . but for Sam *Sneder*, 3 Maple Drive, Apt. #10, New York, NY 10021. But for the Publisher's Clearinghouse sweepstakes, you send in the card from Sam *Sleder*, 3 Maple Drive, Apt. #15, New York, NY 10021.

And on and on and on. Slowly but surely, you're creating a world of near-clones, slightly imperfect beings whose ultimate role is to collectively baffle the privacy-invading SOBs who will soon (don't forget) be coming for you.

### Give Yourself Some Credit: Lots of It

This is similar to step 1—only this time, with credit card applications. You're not going to be applying for one new credit card, my friend, nor for two or three. We're talking about thirty cards, forty cards, a hundred cards. American Express, Visa, Player's Club, Exxon, whatever. Get yourself a Bloomingdale's card, a Sears card, a Target card. (Do they have Target cards? Something tells us they probably do.) You know that card that your alma mater keeps offering, the MasterCard with a picture of the quad on it? Now's the time to get it.

Don't stop applying, even when you say to yourself, haven't I applied for enough? How much credit does one person need? But the point here isn't credit—it's getting as many versions of yourself out there as possible.

Do you like kicking back on Sundays and reading the *New York Times*? Big waste of time. Instead, take an hour or two each Sunday applying for credit cards. You only want no-fee cards. Why? Because you want to pay no fee. For cards seeking a fee, just send them an empty envelope, or, better yet, several pieces of heavyweight construction board—they have to pay for the postage. Nothing like sticking it to corporate loan sharks.

Just be sure not to forget the key factor here—as you did with your junk mail returns in step 1, you should be getting little details wrong on each of these credit card applications. Here you want to focus on your Social Security number; maybe that 9 comes out looking like a 1, because the loop part didn't come out just right. Not your fault. Maybe your 2 has something of a 3-ish quality to it, at least enough so that the well-meaning data-entry clerk in Pakistan or Bangladesh (or wherever American Express has outsourced its data-entry mines to) makes a small error. Perhaps Stephen Sherrill becomes Stephen Sherri. You get the picture.

Now, 90 percent of these little "noise" creators will get rejected, but those remaining 10 percent . . . Voilà! You've got more near-clones out there in the data universe. You the Reader are now getting lost among all the You the Neaders! Oh, and hang on to those cards—you'll need them later.

## Build Up Your Calf Muscles
Stand on your toes. Tiptoe across your apartment. Flex your calves as you walk upstairs. Get that look off your face—just do it.

## Welcome to the Fascinating World of Numismatics
It's bank-account time. Here, you're going to have to use your real name and info—banks are picky. You're also going to have to pay some fees—but it's a small price to pay for buying yourself a head start on the dogs. You want to get as many ATM cards as possible from as many different banking institutions as possible. Now, you're also going to have to deposit cash in these accounts. This may be a bit tricky, because living under the Bush economy, you likely won't have much, but scrape up what you can.

Now tally up all your funds. Then put them into two piles.

Pile 1 should be 80 percent of your cash. Pile 2, 20 percent. Take pile 1 and stick it in or under your mattress. Also, you may want to convert that cash into euros—if you keep it in dollars for longer than a couple of months, it may end up being worthless.

(Note: Actually switching currencies too much will probably draw notice, so buy one of those coin-collector sets. You're not preparing to flee the country, you're just a numismatics enthusiast! [Wink, wink.] In fact, maybe you should also get into some other eccentric hobbies, like stamp collecting [philately] and *Star Trek* action-figure trading, just to balance things out.

And don't worry—those action figures will retain their value more than the U.S. dollar. Now that we mention it, in general, you should be a little more idiosyncratic—a lovable eccentric—what you want is for people to say you're an odd duck, a real "character.")

Now, pile 2. Deposit this cash in your various bank accounts in increments ending with a 3, 5, or 7—for no other reason than it looks like a pattern. Don't forget to get your ATM cards!

### Get Lots of Cell Phones

Cheap ones. From lots of different carriers. With a variety of numbers (make a game of requesting different numbers—like 212-555-BUTT or whatever—going underground should be a fun experience). Another side benefit is your chance to test out definitively which of these companies actually gets you best reception. Plus, you'll look like a rap star.

### How Are Those Calf Muscles Coming Along?

Just keep flexing. And take the stairs, you sissy.

### Book a Different Trip Every Month

Go online, pick a destination—the Caribbean, Indonesia, even Canada. Then find a chain hotel, book yourself a room for two months from now. Wait a week, cancel it. Man is that idiosyncratic! What are You the Reader up to? I don't know. Nobody does. You're an odd duck!

### Calves? Good?

Maybe you want to shave them. No reason.

*Phone Book Phun!*
This is the part where you look for random names and addresses of people you don't know in states all across the country; make yourself a nice list.

*The Day Will Come*
But why? Why will it come?

Maybe they're coming for you because you bought this book or one like it.

If it was this one, sorry. Hope you're a quick reader. No refunds.

Maybe it's that Che Guevara poster you were storing for your college-bound brother. Commies are not okay. Dark-skinned commies are really not okay.

Maybe it was that time you took the Lord Thy God's name in vain . . . in public!

Don't know what we're talking about? Remember when you went to the hardware store, they didn't have the kind of rake you wanted, and you said "Jeez Louise"? What do you think "jeez" is short for? That counts.

Maybe someone saw your wife talking back to you (or walking in stride with you) in the supermarket.

Maybe you went to France, or maybe you just ordered french fries instead of "freedom fries."

Or maybe when they didn't have your rake at the hardware store, and you said "fuck" and then said "Pardon my French." Double whammy!

Maybe you're a Jew.

Maybe you're black.

Maybe you're gay.

If you're a gay black Jew, it's probably too late—they got you already.

Maybe your kid didn't say the Pledge of Allegiance loud enough at school.

Maybe you were talking sports with a buddy and mentioned how well the Red Sox have "evolved" over the last few seasons, et cetera, et cetera.

When will they come for you?

You can't really know when they'll come for you; however, you need to go before they come a-knockin'. It's a dilemma. The solution—as soon as you've followed the steps listed above—hit the highway! Sorry, no one said life on the outskirts of society was going to be easy.

But first, it's time to say good-bye to your loved ones, if they haven't been taken away yet. In fact, you might want to start saying good-bye to your loved ones now, just so you don't have to spend your last twenty-four hours of freedom on the phone. A helpful hint: start with your less-loved ones. Call your aunts and uncles first, work your way up to your parents and your wife, husband, or whatever. Actually, get in the habit of ending every conversation with "Farewell, my friend . . . farewell. I love you."

"What?"

"Oh, nothing."

## TIME TO GO!
Now it's time to boogie—what do I do now?

### Start Sending Letters
Remember all those people whose names you picked out of the phone book? From all over the country? (See Phone Book Phun, above.) Ideally, you sent out around twenty-five to fifty letters. This is where all those credit cards you applied for come into play.

Send a letter to each of them: "Hi! Congratulations—my name is SAM SNEDLER and you are a recipient of the SAM SNEDLER one-time-only scholarship award program. Enclosed please find a credit card for your personal use. Knock yourself out!"

Encourage your "prize winners" to use their cards liberally (no pun intended—that can get you in trouble): "Can we recommend that you buy a trip somewhere? Take yourself to a fancy meal? The ONLY thing required of Sam Snedler scholarship recipients is that you write in this name in the signature card. An exact replica of the signature is below. Oh, and here's the billing zip code and Social Security number. Enjoy your prize! Praise Jesus."

But wait! Why would someone use a free credit card that someone sent to them in the mail? Seriously? Because we're fucking Americans!

*ARE YOU GETTING AN INKLING OF OUR STRATEGY HERE? YOU'RE NOT ACTUALLY GOING TO DISAPPEAR—YOU'RE SIMPLY GOING TO HIDE IN A FOREST OF FIDUCIARY CLONES!*

GIVE THE CELL PHONES AND YOUR ATM CARDS TO HOMELESS PEOPLE
No, not homeless charities—actual homeless people. This should be easy—thanks to the economic policies of the Republican Congress, homeless people are everywhere. Be sure to give them your PIN numbers for those ATM cards. (Choosing ones that are ambulatory doesn't hurt.) You've committed an act of charity and you've bought yourself at least a week, since "You the Reader" are still in your hometown, spending cash and chatting away!

*How Do You Get Out of Town . . . And Where Do You Go?*
SWEET CALVES
The best and only way to get out of town, now that you've laid all appropriate groundwork, is via bicycle. You're both (a) minimizing your use of traceable technology, and (b) hiding as you ride your bike—chances are you're nowhere at any given time. The last thing they're looking for is someone riding a bike. After all, you can't take a car. You can't take a plane.* You can't take a train. (Amtrak gives its passenger lists to the DEA.)†

ROUTE CHOICE
We're talking side roads, gullies, in and out of ravines . . . anything that might bring you into contact with suspicious fellow humans is out. Ride as fast as you can, using your monstrous calves. Zigzag your way south. There's no particular reason to go south, except as long as you're escaping privacy

---

* "DEA's Crazytrain," Joel Miller, WorldNetDaily, April 17, 2001.
† "Delta Gives Passenger List to Gov't to Prevent Disease Spread," Associated Press, April 6, 2005.

invasion and religious fundamentalism, you might as well go somewhere with nice weather.

*Enjoy Your New Life!*
You did it! Head down to Venezuela, change your name, and relax. Well, relax until they finally manage to overthrow Hugo Chávez for nationalizing Venezuelan oil and being democratically elected.

# APPENDIX

As listeners of Air America's *Majority Report* know, Sam's cohost on the show is a woman named Janeane Garofalo. For those who only know Janeane through her work of Entertaining America Through the Magic of Hollywood, Janeane qua* Janeane has many opinions on many things. Opinions that she will share with you. And now she is about to share some of her opinions on this book.

So here now are a few words to start your journey, from a great American and "funny lady" in her own right, the *Majority Report*'s—America's—Janeane Garofalo.

* * *

## RINGING DENUNCIATION, BY JANEANE GAROFALO

Hello, my name is Janeane Garofalo. Let me start by taking issue with almost everything the authors have written. Especially the book's title: *F.U.B.A.R.* Not only is the acronym crass,† but it's also inaccurate. When it comes to military conflicts, "fucked up" situations are both common and recognizable. (Hence all the memoirs, movies, memorials, protests, disinformation, complaints, and casualties.)

Next, there's the application of the term *F.U.B.A.R.* to the right wing, and with it the authors' implication that the right in this country has

---

* We just learned what this means, and still are not entirely sure about it, but we do know it sounds smart.

† Crass can be okay, but only if the writer is far more eloquent and charismatic than Sam Seder.

somehow "changed" from what they once were. To that, I'd say the right's absolutist, fear-based, uncharitable mind-set has always been obvious. Their brand of overt cruelty, belligerence, paranoia, and crap journalism consistently presents itself in the form of unexamined patriotism, Holy War, Anglo-American masculinity, lack of critical thinking, sectarianism, and, of course, bumper stickers.

The authors, by claiming to "wake" you, the reader, imply that you are somehow complicit in allowing the domination by the Rapture Right. This assignment of blame is woefully misplaced. Sam and Stephen might as well say you were "asking for it." Hey, you must have wanted it—what with that short skirt and filthy red lipstick. You know how right-wingers are—they see that outfit and those shoes and: BAM! It's all over but the privatization and homophobia.

I will say, however, that their categorization of me as a "great American" and a "funny lady in her own right" is, in a word, absolutely correct. Though the term "funny lady" is a bit antiquated and anachronistic, but, then, Sam is also a bit antiquated and anachronistic, which explains why he and his unrelenting cabal of holiday-hating Jews are always trying to steal Christmas.

Yours,
Janeane Q. Garofalo, Esq.

# ACKNOWLEDGMENTS

The authors wish to thank—or, depending on you look at it, blame—the following people for their help and encouragement in making *F.U.B.A.R.* possible.

First, there's our editor at HarperCollins, David Hirshey, not just for his dedicated editorial guidance but for starting the whole thing, and then, much to our chagrin, refusing to forget that we'd all agreed to it. Also to Nick Trautwein at HarperCollins, for his editing prowess on the manuscript and for his ability to be patient and stern at the same time.

For their excellent research, we'd like to thank Stephen Hach, Colin Sterling, and Ben Winters.

Among the many friends who helped with their encouragement, suggestions, political talk, and tolerance for listening to whatever latest outrage we'd discovered, we're grateful to Ellen Abrams, Eric Anderson, Kevin Baker, Josh Bearman, Jim Biederman, Zev Borow, Roger Burlingame, Glen Caplin, Michael Cavadias, Dave Derby, Deirdre Dolan, Dan Dratch, Stephen Elliott, Sarah Geary, Tim Geary, Malcolm Gladwell, Tom Hackett, Cate Hartley, Kevin Hench, Dave Hill, Jack Hitt, Heather Juergensen, Joan Levine, David Lipsky, Joel Lovell, Sara Mosle, Kate Porterfield, Hannah Rosin, Lisa Sanders, Tom Scharpling (the godfather of "The Majority Report"), Bill Scher, Evie Shapiro, Paul Tough, Sarah Vowell, Jonathan Walsh, John Williams, and, especially, for her repeated manuscript readings and improvements, Susan Lehman.

Much of the source material for the book came from our favorite blogs, all of which we recommend: AMERICAblog, Crooks and Liars, Cursor, Daily Kos, Eschaton, Firedoglake, First Draft, Steve Gilliard's The News Blog, Huffington Post, Hullabaloo, MyDD, Talking Points Memo, and The Washington Note.

Thanks, too, for his contributions and his golden voice, to Jon Benjamin, the signature announcer of "The Majority Report," and to the Seder family for consistently listening to the show and only rarely criticizing Sam.

Thanks also to our agents, Richard Abate (Sam) and David McCormick (Stephen), as well as Leslie Falk.

And also to Mitch Kaplan, Bob Gumer, and Cheryl Stanley for their patience and support.

We want to thank Air America Radio, not least for its lax supervision of office supplies, and our past and present colleagues at "The Majority Report": Isaac Aronson, Mark Hatch-Miller, Logan Nakyanzi, and, especially, Josh Orton, for his valuable editorial input and his irrational but touching and continuing belief in Thomas Friedman.

Thanks to all in the administration of Air America Radio, including but not limited to Carl Ginsburg, Doug Kreeger, and Jon Sinton, who were busy saving AAR when we were planning this book. And to Danny Goldberg and Gary Krantz for sustaining the network, and, in advance, for all the free advertisements they'll surely offer us to promote *F.U.B.A.R.*, as well as Jaime Horn, Mike Malloy, John Manzo, Andi Parhamovich, Colin Tipton, Andy Yako-Mink, and Justin Yuen.

And, of course, to Yaddo, MacDowell, and the MacArthur Foundation, for not bothering us with annoying offers of fellowships and awards while we were busy writing.

Last but not least, thanks to George Bush, Dick Cheney, Tom Delay, James Dobson, Bill Frist, and Rick Santorum. Without their tireless efforts, none of this would have been possible.